ISBN: 9781407797342

Published by:
HardPress Publishing
8345 NW 66TH ST #2561
MIAMI FL 33166-2626

Email: info@hardpress.net
Web: http://www.hardpress.net

NO GAINS WITHOUT PAINS.

A

TRUE LIFE FOR THE BOYS.

BY H. C. KNIGHT.

PUBLISHED BY THE
AMERICAN TRACT SOCIETY,
150 NASSAU-STREET, NEW YORK.

CONTENTS.

CHAPTER I

CHAPTER II.

CHAPTER III.

CHAPTER IV.

CHAPTER V.

NO PAINS, NO GAINS.

CHAPTER I.

THE OLD HORSESHOE—LITTLE DONKEY—THE MOTHER'S PRAYER.

ONE day a little boy on his way to school picked up an old horseshoe. What did he do with it? He carried it three miles to a blacksmith's shop, and sold it for a penny. It was the first penny he ever had. "No gains without pains," perhaps he thought. He did not directly go and spend it. He laid it by; and we will see how he added to it. A short time afterwards, a man who had been watching a boy carrying dirt from his father's door, called Samuel, for that was our little boy's name, and told him if he would beat that boy in carrying dirt, he would give him a penny. Samuel tried his hand, and earned the wages.

"Now," said the man, "if you will show me this same penny in a fortnight, I will give you another; and I will make a mark on it, so as to know it." He marked and gave it to Samuel, for I suppose he knew how boys like to spend, and he had a mind to try Samuel on this point. In a fortnight he showed the man the penny. "There it is, sir," said he.

"Good," said the man; "you shall have another; you know how to keep, as well as to earn." Samuel now had three pennies. An English penny is two of our cents. He was, therefore, according to our currency, worth six cents. Perhaps you would like to know a little more of his earnings. One day, one of his sisters, in drawing molasses, let a quantity run over the kettle she was filling on to the floor. She took up all she supposed worth saving, and was about to wash up the rest, when Samuel asked if *he* might not have it; and on his sister's giving him leave, he carefully scraped it up, and sold it for three half-pence. How many cents is that? Three cents: he has now, then, nine cents.

"No gains without pains," Samuel thought, or at least he acted upon the principle, if a penny was worth having, it was worth the trouble of earning. I am afraid all boys do not think so. They like the penny, but are not willing to work for it; and therefore some boys are tempted to get money in very questionable ways, which are apt to lead to disgrace and ruin.

"What did Samuel do with his money?" some one may have the curiosity to ask. It is pleasant to know what people do with their first earnings. As soon as he had enough, he bought a book with it, a hymn-book; and then he felt as rich and happy as could be.

Samuel lived in England. He was born in the little village of Wrington, ten miles south-west of Bristol, in 1794. Bristol is a large city in the south-western part of England, one hundred and fourteen miles west of London. When Samuel was seven, his parents moved to Kingswood, a village on the edge of Bristol; and as this was the place where his life was spent, I must stop in the story, and tell you a little about Kingswood.

In old times it was indeed, what its name

signifies, a king's wood; for it was a tract of
three or four thousand acres of land, used by
the king and his nobles for a royal hunting-
ground. Besides the wild beasts which roamed
in this forest, there was a set of wild, lawless
men, called foresters, who had their haunts in
it. They were a terror to the country around,
for they lived by plunder and robbery, and it
was often dangerous for travellers, unarmed
and alone, to be found near this wood after
nightfall. But in the course of years, the deer
had gradually disappeared, and the forest and
the foresters. The reputation of the place,
however, had not much improved. The land
had been turned to better account; for coal-
mines had been discovered, which supplied
Bristol and the neighboring towns with fuel,
and supported a large population of colliers—
men who work the coal-pits—who had gradually settled on the soil. Their cottages had
been put up without much regard to order,
here and there and everywhere; so that unless
very familiar, in trying to find the way among
them, one was quite sure to lose it among the
endless number of narrow lanes: crooked, turning, winding, crossing, and branching off in all

directions. It was indeed a jumble of a town, if it could be called a town. And the people were as disorderly as their houses were. Bad as the foresters had been, the colliers could beat them in wickedness. A more ferocious and brutal set of men never disgraced a Christian land.

When the famous preacher WHITEFIELD was at Bristol, in 1739, and talked of coming to this country to convert the Indians, some people said, "What is the need of going abroad for this object? Have we not savages enough at home? If you have a mind to convert Indians, there are colliers enough in Kingswood."

These remarks made a deep impression upon the mind of this good man. He could not turn from his own countrymen. And when he rode over to Kingswood, and saw what the state of the people really was, he felt his bowels yearn over them, for he saw them as sheep without a shepherd, given over to the devouring wolves of sin and Satan. Nobody had cared for their souls. They had no schools, no churches, no Bibles, no preachers, no prayers. Sunk in degradation and dirt, people seemed to think nothing could be done to improve their condition;

and although on the edge of a great Christian city, Bristol, they had been left year after year, and generation after generation, to grow up and die in their wickedness.

But when Whitefield came, and Wesley, and their pious coadjutors, a new and better day broke upon the darkness of Kingswood; and the success of their labors at Kingswood proved that no people are too low or too hardened to welcome the faithful preaching of the gospel of Jesus Christ.

"Yes," said Whitefield, first on the field, "something can and must be done for these poor people; the Lord Jesus Christ came into this world to seek and to save the lost; if so, the Kingswood colliers are just the people to be saved."

In this spirit he went one afternoon over to the collieries; it was on Saturday, February 17, 1737, and a memorable day, because it was the first day the gospel was ever preached there. His church was the open air, and his pulpit a little mound of earth. About two hundred men, women, and children gathered gapingly around to listen. "Who is he?" "What does this mean?" they asked one of another. "What is he telling about? And they run out of their cottages and stared and hearkened.

How much they understood the first day I cannot tell, but it is certain that they were interested and pleased. His bright eye and beaming countenance, the clear, sweet tones of his voice, ringing in their ears words of love and mercy, words of God and heaven and hell, did not fail to attract them. He must have seemed like some superior being come on an errand of good. And as he passed by, his kind look and friendly notice of one and another drew hearts towards him. How they looked wonderingly after him until out of sight; in how many cottages and ale-houses was he talked over that night.

A *beginning of good* was then and there made at Kingswood. How did it go on? On White-field's second visit, two thousand people throng-ed to hear him. On his third visit, from four to five thousand.

"The trees and hedges were full," he said; "all was a hush when I began; the sun shone bright, and God enabled me to preach over an hour with great power, and so loud that all

could hear me. Blessed be God! To behold
such crowds standing together in such awful
silence, and to hear their singing run from one
end to the other, was very solemn and striking."
"And how was I affected," he again says,
"when I saw the white gutters made by the
tears which plentifully fell down their black
faces—black as they came out of their coal-
pits."

The poor colliers showed they had hearts to
feel the force of Bible truths. And the more
they heard, the more they wanted to hear.
Sometimes ten, fifteen, and twenty thousand
people are said to have crowded around this
remarkable preacher during his field-preaching
at Kingswood. Many, I suppose, came from
Bristol in their carriages, and on horseback.
Many, like Zaccheus, climbed up into the trees.
On all sides they pressed to hear him.

Mr. Whitefield, loath to leave this interesting
and important field of labor, and yet under the
necessity of leaving to meet engagements elsewhere, wrote to his friend John Wesley, begging him to hasten to Bristol. Wesley obeyed
the call, and came without delay. Preaching
in the open air, or field-preaching, as it is called,

was something altogether new, and what Wesley had never yet seen. He was not sure whether he could approve of it. It seemed to him a breach of order and propriety. But when he saw how people were hungering for the truth, and that no church could hold the multitudes eager to hear, he was thankful for *any* opportunity of preaching to them Jesus Christ the Saviour of sinners.

Besides, he remembered how his Lord had delivered his sermon on the mount. Accordingly, the next day he followed the example of his friend. He went out into a field, and preached to a congregation of three thousand. It was something he never was sorry for. "I have since seen," he tells us, "abundant reason to adore the wise providence of God herein, making a way for myriads of people who never troubled any church, and are never likely to do so, to hear that word, which they soon found to be the power of God unto their salvation."

But something more than preaching was necessary. The children must be cared for—the "dear lambs," as Whitefield calls them. Could not a school be set up? This Whitefield proposed to the colliers. The poor men were much pleased, and promised to help by their money or their work, and they begged him to stay and lay the corner-stone of a new building for that purpose. It did not seem very clear where the money was to come from, for people were not as ready to give their money for charitable objects then as they now are; but both Whitefield and Wesley had a great deal of faith and courage. They acted much upon the principle, Where there is a will, there is a way; and therefore they determined to lay the foundation-stone of the new school, and then to lay plans to build upon it.

. Did their preaching produce much effect? "By the grace of God, their labor was not in vain," says an eye-witness of the change. "Kingswood does not now, as a year ago, resound with cursing and with blasphemy. It is no more filled with drunkenness and uncleanness, and the idle diversions they lead to. It is no longer full of wars and fightings, of clamor and bitterness, of wrath and envyings. Peace and love are there. Great numbers of the people are gentle, mild, and easy to be entreated. They do not 'cry, neither strive,' and hardly is their voice heard in the streets, or indeed in their own ward, unless when they are at their usual evening devotions, singing praises unto God their Saviour."   .

Whitefield soon after left to visit the United States. The home mission thus begun at Kingswood, was carried on by Wesley, and afterwards by his successors.   .

A marked reformation took place : but great and noticeable as it was, a great deal of patient, spiritual husbandry was necessary to perfect the fruit, and especially to take care of the little seeds and shoots of divine grace, and to renew the seeds, and to weed the soil, and nurture the young plants, and to bring forth a harvest that should honor God. The bad habits and wrong opinions of a large community cannot be broken up in a day or a year, and good habits and right notions directly formed. There were still ale-houses. There were secret places where thieves used to bandy together ; and there were reckless, lawless fellows, who of course hated the reformation which they could not prevent, and who tried all they could to hinder the progress of religion among their companions.

Chapels had been built, schools had been

opened, faithful preachers had labored to bring
men to repentance and to walk in the fear of
God ; but when Samuel Budgett and his father's
family moved to Kingswood, there were still
many neighborhoods where wickedness lurked,
and there was work enough for God's people
to do.

The Budgetts were Wesleyan Christians.
They feared God, and tried to bring up their
family to love and serve him. They were poor,
but frugal and industrious, and on coming to
Kingswood, opened a shop on the "cassy," or
causeway. Samuel was seven at the time of
their moving. Here he found the horseshoe,
and here he went to such schools as the neighborhood afforded. How many crumbs of knowledge he picked up we do not know ; but we
find he was twice punished at dame Stone's
school : once for picking up an apple under a
tree, and again for washing his shoe in her pan
of clean water. And what do you think the
punishment was? He was put in a corner, and
had a long, speckled worsted stocking drawn
over his head, with the foot dangling in his
face.

He was afterwards sent to another school,

where the chief instruction of the mistress was telling the children stories about all sorts of hobgoblins; so I think we cannot call his early advantages for schooling very superior; on the contrary, they were very poor. Samuel liked the shop better than school; perhaps he felt he learned more there, for he used to observe very carefully how business was done, and sometimes he ventured upon small bargains on his own responsibility.

One day a woman came into the shop with a basket of cucumbers. Samuel asked the price not only of one, but of her whole stock. His oldest brother Henry, who was in the store, thought him very inquisitive and forward, and I dare say told him to be off. But Samuel said he meant to buy the cucumbers, which he did; he then went and sold them in the neighborhood, and made ninepence on the sale, which is eighteen cents of our money.

A boy-merchant, is he not? Sometimes he bought and sold eggs, chickens, pigs, always with a fair profit, and once a donkey.

He met, one day, a man with an old donkey and a little one. "How much will you take for your little donkey?" asked Samuel, stopping to examine the animals. ".Two shillings and sixpence," answered the man. "It is a bargain, then," said the boy, who paid the man his price, and led the little donkey home. A few days afterwards, a woman offered five shillings for it. She had no money then, she said, but promised to pay him in a week. Not thinking it safe to trust her promise alone, he wanted security. "I have nothing in the world to let you have," said she, "but a pair of stays." "Very well," said Samuel, "I will take them, for they are easily carried." He took them home, and told his mother, when Mrs. Miles brought the money, to give her back the stays. But before the week was out, little donkey died. The woman then wanted her stays back. "No," said the boy, "the bargain was fair. Donkey became your property, and donkey's dying is therefore your loss, not mine." And so I suppose the woman had to redeem her stays with five shillings, or he sold them elsewhere.

Samuel's parents staid but two years at Kingswood, when they gave up the shop to Henry, and moved to Coleford. Henry was Mr. Budgett's child by a former wife, and fifteen years older than Samuel. At Coleford they opened another shop, but business was small, the family large, and it was often difficult to make the two ends of the year meet. Poor as they were in earthly goods, they had riches laid up in heaven; and their trust in God made them thankful and happy with their coarse fare. The Wesleyan preachers were often welcomed to their frugal table, and when they came, Samuel loved dearly to listen to their pious conversation.

When he was nine years old, passing early one morning his mother's chamber, he heard her voice in prayer, and he stopped to listen, for she seemed praying with more than common fervency. And who was she praying for? What had sent her at this early hour of the morning to the throne of God? It was for her son that this mother prayed.

"Oh," cried Samuel, "if my mother is so anxious for my conversion, how anxious ought I to be for it myself!" It struck him to the heart. He went away by himself. He thought over his many, many faults; they never looked so big and so serious and so awful before. He saw how offensive they were in the sight of God. He felt very unhappy. Would he go away and try to forget them; or would he seek, in penitence and prayer, God's forgiveness and favor?

Samuel did not try to forget; he did not want to banish serious thoughts from his mind. He wished to be truly penitent; and he prayed God for his dear Son's sake to forgive him, and to give him a new heart, a heart to hate sin and to love the Saviour, a heart to obey his will and keep his holy laws.

This little boy began on that day to pray, *meaning* his prayer. A great many children pray without minding what they say, or caring whether God hears them; these are "words upon a thoughtless tongue," and such prayer cannot be acceptable to God. If you are very anxious to have a favor granted to you by your father, how carefully and how earnestly you ask it; your manner and your tones are such as show your interest in the matter. You can hardly be put off. Your whole heart is engaged in it. "Please, do," is your earnest cry. This, you know, is the way to gain your father's ear; he will not turn you off; he will hear, and if it is best, how willingly will he grant your request, and give you what you need. But God

is more ready to hear and to answer your cries
for forgiveness and heavenly things, than earthly parents are to give good gifts to their children—*more ready.*

But children sometimes say, I have prayed—
I have prayed a great many times, but God
did not answer me. I have asked him to make
me a penitent, believing child; but alas, I am
not.

Did you pray *in earnest?* Did you *keep on
praying?* Samuel was in earnest; Samuel kept
on praying. And you see how God *answered*
prayer in the case of this mother and her son.
Among all her family cares and labors, what is
the *first thing* this mother wants? Her son's
conversion. That is the most important thing
of all. What is the first duty which the mother
of this large family engages in? It is to pray
God for her son's conversion.

That mother was in earnest. And what
does Jesus say? "Ask, and ye shall receive."
I suppose this mother went to God in simple
and sincere reliance upon the word of his dear
Son. And God was as good as his word. The
mother's prayer fell like a blessing on the little
boy himself as he passed by her door. He went

away, and carried the blessing with him, for
God accompanied it by his Holy Spirit; and
when God blesses, nobody can snatch the good
from us. And what did it do? It did not
harden. It touched and softened him; he shed
tears of penitence for himself, and it excited
him to turn unto God with his whole heart, and
pray for his own salvation. And he became a
child of God. These feelings did not pass
away from his mind, like early dew from the
flowers of the garden. He did not go back to
thoughtlessness and irreligion, as children often
do after they have been awakened to some degree of concern for their souls. He kept on,
for God kept him. "They that seek me early
shall *find* me," is the gracious promise of our
heavenly Father.

Will not other children, and will not moth-
ers also take encouragement from this beautiful
example of Samuel and his mother, and *believe*
in God's *willingness to hear* and to answer
prayer?

There was a poor woman very sick in the
neighborhood about this time, whose happy
experience of the value of religion on a sick
and dying bed strengthened Samuel in his de-

sires to secure it. His mother often visited poor Betty Coles, and on her return used often to describe to the family the comfort and joy which she experienced in her Saviour; and when she died, it seemed only a step from earth to heaven. Samuel thought a great deal about the happy death-bed of this good woman, and he often went out into the fields in the summer evenings to sing to himself the hymns which cheered and comforted her; and as he thought and sung, death lost its terrors, and nothing seemed more desirable to the boy than to go home and live with his Saviour in heaven.

But Samuel did not die young, for God had work for him to do on earth.

His mother in a few months was taken ill, and brought very low. One night she was thought to be dying. Samuel was suddenly called up, old Bob was saddled, and the boy was sent in all haste three miles on a dark winter night for the doctor. A sorrowful ride it must have been. Much as the doctor might be able to do for his mother, Samuel believed God could do far more, therefore he kept praying all the way that her life might be spared, and health again return to her.

On his way back the day began to dawn, and as he was passing Mells park, a little bird struck up a cheerful note just over his head. The bird-song sounded most sweetly to him. It filled him with feelings of joy and gratitude, and seemed almost to assure him that God in mercy would answer his prayer and restore his dear mother to health. On reaching home he could not help exclaiming, "Sister Betsey, mother will get well." "What makes you think so?" she asked. "Oh, I feel that God will spare her ever since I passed Mells park this morning." Sister Betsey saw no good reason for laying aside her fears, I dare say, however the boy might; but this morning's ride was a ride he loved to remember through his whole life, for the experience of *joy* which he had in casting his load of sorrow upon God, and putting his trust in him. God filled his bosom with a sweet peace.

It might seem strange to some, that a poor shivering little boy, on a sorrowful errand like that, on a dark winter morning, far from home, could feel *very happy.* There was certainly nothing in his circumstances to make him happy. Every thing looked as dark and comfort-

less as could be. But when God fills the soul
with *his* joy and *his* peace, then a person will
be happy anywhere, no matter if he is in a
dungeon; for true religion can make a person
happy without the aid of any thing else. This
was a taste of the enjoyment which God's children have. Samuel, by penitence and prayer
and faith, had become God's child; and I am
sure it tasted better than any thing else he
ever had. It is better than any thing father or
mother, or brother or sister, or minister or
friend can give—better than any thing which
the whole world can offer. The whole world
and ten thousand worlds cannot give one drop
of comfort to the soul, like that which God can
give.

One of the old prophets said, "Although the
fig-tree shall not blossom, neither shall fruit be
in the vines; the labor of the olive shall fail,
and the fields shall yield no meat; the flock
shall be cut off from the fold, and there shall
be no herd in the stalls"—a pretty desolate
picture of a famine it is—"yet," he said, not-
withstanding this desolation and want, "I will
rejoice in the Lord, I will joy in the God of my
salvation."

Is not a religion that can give so much of just what the heart craves, the hearts of *children* as well as grown-up people, *genuine happiness* — is not such a religion worth having, worth *making sure of?* Samuel thought so, as we shall see.

Did his mother get well? Yes; and one day when he went to walk with her, he, told her of his sweet experience of God's goodness on his ride by Mells park. And was she not glad?. O yes; for happy indeed are those parents whose children trust in the Lord, fearing him and keeping his law.

CHAPTER II.

WHAT TO DO—LEAVING HOME—THE APPRENTICESHIP.

SAMUEL was now fourteen years old, and the question had often been agitated in the family councils, "what he was going to do." A more serious question than this often comes up about boys of this age, which occasions more perplexity and many more anxious days to decide; it is this, "What is the boy going *to be?*" That is the greatest question, *What is he going to be?* A weak, thriftless, irresponsible man; or a prompt, energetic, reliable one? An industrious, painstaking, God-fearing man; or an idle, slovenly, irreligious one? A man worth something, or a man worth nothing? A poet says, "The boy is father of the man;" which means, that the germs of the future man are growing in the boy. The seeds of future character are no doubt there, and it is precisely this which makes the tastes, tendencies, and habits of boyhood a matter of such weighty concern to parents. What the boy is going to *do*, is second to what he is going to *be ;* for what he *does*, will very greatly depend upon what *he is.*

It is not so impórtant what kind of business a man engages in, provided it is an honest one, as upon what principles it is conducted—how much energy, prudence, foresight, and prayer he throws into it. It is upon *such* foundations that true success is built. It is such elements which make business *good*—good for the master, good for his men, good for the community in which he lives.

By the time Samuel was fourteen, the question what he was going *to be,* occasioned no anxiety in the minds of his parents; that was pretty nearly decided, although every body, perhaps, did not discern the real merits of the little fellow. But what was he going to *do?* Samuel had a choice in the matter. He wanted to become a missionary, he longed to preach the gospel. That was his strong desire, one day to be a preacher. He was not, however, too young to see there were many serious obstacles in the way. He was poor, and poorly educated even in the branches of a common education; then he doubted his capacity: he hardly thought he had talent fit for such an office. Besides, his parents needed help, and was it not his duty to qualify himself to assist them as soon as possible?

Many days and nights he pondered this question of duty. One day as he was riding along on his father's horse thinking these matters over, he fell to musing, and imagined himself transported to some foreign land as a missionary, engaged in preaching the gospel to the heathen; and he almost fancied himself kneeling under the bushes and among the rocks, drawing down blessings by faith and prayer. For a time he forgot where he was. And when at last he awoke from his dream, he found the bridle loose on the horse's neck, and the horse standing under a large tree in a lane, eating grass. It appeared to him that for some time he had been surrounded by a great congregation, whom he had been begging to flee from the wrath to come, and who accepted salvation through Jesus Christ. One thing was certain, he had been weeping a great deal, for the pommel of his saddle and the horse's shoulders were wet with his tears; and he rode home with a sweet feeling of peace such as could not be described.

Then the uppermost thought was to give up all idea of trade, and devote himself to study for the gospel ministry.

But a different path lay out before him. And the final decision was, that he should go into his brother Henry's store at Kingswood, and serve with him a regular apprenticeship of seven years.

Samuel had laid up at this time the sum of thirty pounds, the fruit of his own earnings and savings—a handsome sum for a boy of his age to be master of. Now, what do you suppose he did with it? Invested in bank-stock at six per cent., it would have been a nice little capital to have started business with at twenty-one. He did invest it, but not in bank-stock. On leaving home, he made a present of it to his mother. And he always considered it the best investment he ever made, for he says, "*No investment under the sky is so sure as a parent's blessing.*"

Let the boys think of that. It should be written in letters of gold. "There is no investment under the sky so *sure* as a parent's blessing."

With such a parting gift to his dear mother,

Samuel started for Kingswood. His brother's shop was a variety-store, containing almost every thing which might be wanted in the families of the colliers. It was called the "great shop on the cassy." · All around were the rude and humble houses of the collier population. Some were thrifty and comfortable, others poor and comfortless; the people, as a class, were ignorant and degraded; there were many circumstances which hindered their moral and social improvement, and nourished the worst passions of the human heart. Almost in the immediate neighborhood were nests of robbers, who prowled by night around the farms and hamlets of the vicinity, and stole whatever they could lay their hands on. Many a time, when the farmers and constables were searching their premises for stolen goods, the thieves would show them their own pigs and poultry, dead and picked, and defy them to prove their property.

This was home heathenism. If Samuel therefore wanted opportunities to do missionary work, Kingswood offered ample room for all labors of the kind. Indeed, every young person with a heart to do good, can find a great

deal of good to do not very far from his own
door.

Samuel soon found his hands full of shop-
work, from morning till night, all the week.
By six in the morning he, was expected to be on
duty, and often his labors were not closed until
ten or eleven at night. The work was very
hard ; there was a great deal of heavy lifting,
and many errands to be done in Bristol, requir-
ing a swift foot. It was work, work, work,
with hardly interval enough for rest, or any
leisure to improve his mind by reading, except
on Sunday, and Sunday was a welcome and
precious day to poor Samuel. Its sacred hours
he highly prized ; its opportunities for improvement he diligently cultivated.

There was a little chapel close by his brother's, where the family worshipped ; and there
Samuel used to go every Sabbath morning, eager
to hear the preaching, and delighted to engage
in the devotions of the people of God. The
sermons were a great treat to him, and lest he
should forget any thing by the way, or have his
mind diverted from the truth by hearing foolish
or unprofitable talk, he often stopped his ears
on his way home. In pleasant weather he

would betake himself to the solitude of an old quarry behind the house, and there, seated upon a piece of slag, would review the sermon, study his Bible,—and learn sacred poetry, striving to store up treasures of divine truth to feed his soul upon during the week.   No gains without pains, Samuel felt, in heavenly as well as in earthly gettings.

I am sure Samuel must have been a good boy—faithful and diligent you are ready to believe.   But for some cause or other he failed to satisfy his brother; and his brother, after two or three years' trial, gave him notice to quit, allowing him a month to look out for another situation.   It was a heavy blow to the poor boy.   What could he do?   If his brother turned him away, what reasonable expectation was there of his getting another place?   He however heard of a vacancy in a store in Bristol, and resolved to apply for it without delay. When he reached the door, his heart failed him, for he knew his size and appearance and clothes were all against him.   Samuel was small of his age, and not very stout.   Plucking up courage, he ventured in, and offered his services.

"I am afraid you are not strong enough for my situation," said the shop-keeper.

"O do try me, sir; I am sure I can do," said the boy.

"Can you write your address?" asked Mr. B——.

Samuel was not quite sure what "address" meant, but he said, "I can write an invoice, sir." Do the boys who read this know what "invoice" means?

"Very well," said the shop-keeper, "write eighty-six pounds of bacon, at nine and a half pence per pound."

Samuel wrote it, but the reckoning was wrong. He tried a second time, and failed. How badly he felt. Just then a young man, tall and well-dressed, entered the shop on the same errand for which Samuel was on trial. What hope was there for him? The shop-keeper's wife, however, was pleased with the boy's looks, and she urged a word in his favor.

"He is not strong enough," said the shop-keeper; "he could never carry those heavy cheeses."

"Do try me, sir," pleaded Samuel; "I am sure I can do it." And instantly going to work among the cheeses, he showed so much spirit that the man concluded to take him.

He was dismissed from his brother's store on the score of "want of ability," as was found recorded on Henry's books. The result will show that masters may be mistaken in the capacities of their apprentices, and that boys, even if they do their best, need not be discouraged if they fail to suit their first employers.

Before going to Bristol, he determined to pay his parents a visit at Coleford, and a younger brother, who was an apprentice in Bristol, got leave to go with him. Leaving Kingswood under such circumstances, was a sore trial to poor Samuel. He felt it something in the light of a disgrace. Before leaving, he asked his brother for a character, for I suppose he was conscious of having done as well as he could. Henry gave him one. At first he was afraid to open the paper and look at it, but turning into a little gate by the roadside to hide his agitation, he ventured to peep in, and was greatly relieved to find his want of strength given as a reason for his dismissal.

The boys started on their journey on foot. And how do you suppose they employed their time? The younger brother had been at better schools, and his stock of learning, small as it probably was, was superior to Samuel's. Samuel therefore determined to take advantage of his brother's knowledge; and as they travelled, they practised addition, multiplication, and division on all the bacon, butter, cheese, and chickens they could think of. Samuel was anxious to become a ready and accurate reckoner, and a persevering use of even *his* slender advantages he well knew would increase his skill. "No gains without pains," was his maxim.

The boys were so much interested in their arithmetic, that they lost their reckoning of the road. Night overtook them far from Coleford, but near the friendly warmth of a coke-kiln; and tired enough, they concluded to lie down and pass the night by the fire. Early the next morning, a cartman passing that way, offered the boys a ride, which they were very thankful to accept, for the ride carried them home in good season for breakfast.

A family meeting as happy as unexpected, it no doubt was. The boys had much to tell, their parents much to hear, and the little children many questions to ask. If Samuel's pleasure was at all damped, and I suppose it was by his brother's course, it received a farther check by the signs of hard times which he saw at home. His father, some years older than his mother, was well along in life, and perhaps could do little for the family maintenance. Poverty sometimes pinched. He was afraid that the struggle must sometimes be severe, and he felt deeply for his mother, whose cares and labors were outrunning her strength. How he longed to be in a situation to help her; how he longed to lift from her the load of care, and place her in ease and comfort. Samuel's courage revived. He was determined to do his best. He would, God willing, *be something*. His resolution took a fresh start. His affections fired up all the energy of his character, and after a few days' visit, he left Coleford to try his fortune in Bristol.

On the journey back, he met a man with a jay to sell. The pretty bird attracted his notice, and he bought it for six cents. Having a few hours to spare after reaching Bristol, he took his stand on the bridge where there were many passers-by, and offered his jay for sale. Nobody seemed disposed to buy. The day was wearing away, and the bird unsold. He then left his stand, and offered it from house to house; this succeeded, and he sold it at a profit of eighteen cents. "No gains, without pains," Samuel thought.

The next morning he went to his new master. Both the man and his wife received him kindly. They soon discovered his worth, and prized his services. Samuel was greatly encouraged, and very happy was he with these good people. While in his brother's employment, he had no opportunity of earning any thing extra for himself. But by some means or other, we find him at this time the possessor of fifteen shillings, which is nearly four dollars of our money. You remember how he invested his thirty pounds. Perhaps you would like also to know how he disposed of this.

Two of his sisters came to live in Bristol; they were trying to maintain themselves, perhaps by sewing, and Samuel, of course, was desirous to lend them a helping hand. One day he went to a coal-pit, and laid out all his money in coal, to be carted to his sisters' lodgings. So ready was he to answer the calls of family affection.

In Mr. Arthur's life of Samuel Budgett there are some remarks upon earning and giving money, which I want every one who reads this to have the benefit of. Rev. Mr. Arthur is an English gentleman, who wrote a large and interesting book called "The Successful Merchant," which I hope you will get and read. He says John Wesley, in a powerful sermon on the use of money, lays down these three rules: "Make all you can; save all you can; give all you can." Both from natural disposition and early habit, Samuel seemed when a boy to understand and act upon these principles, whether he had then ever heard the sermon or not. To make, to save, to give, he set himself. To make without saving, is useless and absurd; to save without giving, is *miserly*; to make and then save, is wise; to save and then give, is Christian.

Which did Samuel do? I want you to stop and think about his course, because it is worth remembering. If you ever do business, it is very important to have some definite notions, some clear Christian principles, in regard to the value and the use of money.

He had not been long away from Kingswood

before Henry Budgett was sensible what a loss
he had met with, and what a mistake he had
made, in parting with his brother. He bitterly
regretted it, for nobody could supply his place,
and he was bent upon having him back. Very
naturally Mr. B—— was loath to give Samuel
up, for a better clerk, of his age, he had never
had in his employment. Indeed, he could not
think of parting with him, and was willing to
give him high wages to stay. Very naturally
Samuel was loath to leave. He was thoroughly
appreciated, had received great kindness, and
was very happy in his Bristol home.

But Henry urged that it was his *duty* to
serve out his apprenticeship, according to the
old agreement; and Samuel, always tender
and scrupulous on every point of duty and conscience, yielded at last to this argument—if
sound argument it was, for his dismissal would
seem to relieve him from any thing like moral
obligation to return. In doing so, he gave up
a good salary for a bare support until the close
of his legal stay, at twenty-one.

Samuel then went back to the old shop in
Kingswood, for which perhaps he felt a linger-
ing affection; for his parents first opened it, and

there he spent some of the most interesting days of his childhood.. He was now about eighteen. If his brother was glad of his return, the customers certainly were also : he was so obliging, so attentive, so anxious to do the best for you ; there was so much *heart* in every thing he did. The old market-women rather wait a long time in order to be served by him ; indeed, they thought he gave better weight and measure than any body else. The people all around loved him as a son and brother. Many a choice apple and bunch of gooseberries from nice little gardens were brought to him. And very grateful was he for these little gifts, but he never ate them : they were delicacies which he denied himself, and hoarded up to take over to a poor old pious aunt living in Bristol ; so thoughtful and interested was he in the *smallest things* which could administer to the comfort and gratification of others.

Whatever Samuel did, he did with his might. All the minute details of business he carefully and faithfully attended to. No slipshod, half-way work ever came from his hands. He always used to say, in whatever calling a Christian is found, he should strive to be the *best* in his calling: if only a shoeblack, he ought to be the best shoeblack in the neighborhood.

The apostle sums up this principle in a short verse, which is of amazing value; it is this, "Whatsoever you do, do it *heartily*, as unto the Lord." These few words are charged with a great deal of hidden power.

You know how much more circumspectly children behave, and how much more faithfully they do their work, if they know their parents are looking on. What energy a boy often throws into his studies, if he feels that the teacher's eye is fixed upon him. And so, with what diligence, what fidelity, what painstaking are those likely to enter upon their work who truly feel that God gave it to them to do, and that he is constantly minding just how they do it.

On Samuel's return to Kingswood, his missionary zeal found an outlet, and we are thankful to follow him into more direct efforts to do good in the neighborhoods around him. I told you about a nest of thieves not very far from Henry Budgett's; they lived at a place called Cockroad, and were called Cockroadites, the terror and dislike of all decent people. And their scores of children were growing up in all the vices of their parents, like the very heathen. Could any thing be done in their behalf? *What* could be done? These were pretty serious questions agitated by the pious people of Kingswood. *Ought* they to be longer neglected? "No, they ought not," said Henry Budgett; "we must make efforts to reclaim them; we must give them the gospel."- It was proposed to establish a Sabbath-school on the spot, and Samuel entered into the plan with all the earnestness of his character. We can readily suppose no person was better suited to visit the parents, and conciliate their good-will, than he. The school was opened in July, 1812; and to their surprise, on the first day seventy-five children made their appearance, fifty-eight of whom did not know their alphabet. Was not the effort worth making?

"Many of them," says one of the teachers, "are children of the notorious tribe of Cockroadites, some of whose fathers are now in prison; and many of them, with their parents, are entirely dependent on a system of robbing and plunder for their support."

Here then was a field of Christian usefulness

demanding patience and prayer, and a true love of souls for Christ's sake. Of children Samuel was very fond. His kind and genial manners won their affections. He entered into their circle of sympathies and interests. He made them his study. He understood how to talk with ,them, and was always on the watch for suitable anecdotes and stories to illustrate and impress the truth. His power over them became very great; and few people could interest audiences of children, hold their attention, and touch their consciences, like Mr. Samuel Budgett. For you remember he acted upon the principle, that every thing worth doing, was worth doing in the best way possible; and although he had had small advantages for education and mental improvement, he became an excellent, devoted, and successful Sabbath-school teacher—one of the best sort. "No gains without pains." No excellence without effort.

Few young men, perhaps, realized more the value of time, and consequently few made a better use of it. How did he learn its value? I will tell you the *principle* upon which this valuation was made ; it is an important one.

"You think," he wrote to a friend, "that if

you were obliged to labor from morning till night, this would teach you the value of time. Is not this a mistake? Can any thing so effectually teach us its value as a deep conviction that it is *not our own*, but an important talent put into our hands, for which we must give a strict account at the great, the general audit of all our accounts with our Maker? If so, of how little importance is it to us what may be the nature or number of our engagements, so long as we may secure at last the blessed plaudit of 'well done' from Him whose approbation alone it is that gives real value to every thing in heaven or earth."

Here is a letter, written towards the close of his apprenticeship, which will help to disclose more of his character.

"KINGSWOOD HILL, August 29.

"MY VERY DEAR FRIEND—Your affectionate letter I received last week. After I had dismissed the business of the day, I retired to my room, sat down, and began to think—How long is it since I received Mr. M——'s book of extracts? How long since he asked me to send him a plan for keeping a commonplace-book? Turning to my little library, Why did I place

so many books on those shelves? I asked. The
feelings of my mind on that occasion I cannot
describe to you ; I believe it was something like
one awaking from a dream who ought to have
been on an important journey some hours before.   I saw that all my powers had been in a
state of dormancy.   I began to reflect on your
past kindness, and considered that I had not
even read all your book, though I intended copy-
ing a great deal of it.   How plainly did I see,
and to my sorrow feel the truth of your obser-
vation, that the mind once enlightened and having lost the love of God, is in a more inactive
state than ever.   I saw that my mind had been
swallowed up in business, to the great neglect
of my spiritual and mental concerns.   I considered that I had been but little different for
seven. years ; and from your letter, I thought
you appeared to be sinking into the same state.
After passing some time—for I took no supper that night, but stayed in my room reason-
ing and endeavoring to think on what had passed till bedtime—I thought, What a deplorable
state we are in.   What can be done?   And I
determined to do something.   I took up my
pen, and wrote down a few little things that I

had neglected, and resolved to execute them in order, and as fast as possible, praying for the blessing of God on my weak endeavors.

"Join with me, my dear friend, join with me in praying that the Lord may add his blessing to my resolutions, and I believe we shall soon see better days. Let us look to that God who has promised, 'I will instruct thee, and teach thee in the way which thou shalt go; I will guide thee with mine eye.' 'I am the light of the world; he that followeth me shall not walk in darkness, but shall have the light of life.' Surely we err in not following him more closely; perhaps we have not thought highly enough of our calling. Let us begin to double our diligence, and henceforth walk as children of the light.

"Inclosed you have a small book with the index to Locke's commonplace-book ruled in it, of which I must beg your acceptance as a small token of my love and affection for you. I have not written a list of my books yet, but hope to do so, and will send it to you in my next.

"As it respects my coming to Frome, I thank you for your kind invitation. I have intended going, but I assure you, when it comes to the point, I have no inclination to go anywhere;

for if I cannot find happiness at home, it is in vain to seek it anywhere else. I think, if I were to come with the determination to enjoy the company of my friends by going to any places of recreation or amusement, though I am very fond of such kind of enjoyments, particularly where religion and real happiness is the subject of conversation, yet it may tend rather to divert my mind from God as the source of my happiness, than unite it to him. But for one thing I have long felt an earnest, though secret desire; which is, to spend a little time with you and Mr. T—— alone, where no object but God could attract our attention; that we may, by devout conversation, by humble, fervent, faithful prayer, get our souls united to each other, and to God our living head, by the strongest ties of love and affection.

"Pray for me, my dear friend. I have only one more request to make; that is, that you will write soon, and believe me your affectionate friend,

"S. B."

This letter is worth many readings. How many young men, young men professing piety, find their own feelings answer to its sentiments?

CHAPTER III.

BUSINESS PRINCIPLES AND HABITS.

WHEN Samuel completed his apprenticeship, and was free, his brother hired him for three years, on a salary of forty pounds for the first year, fifty for the next, and sixty for the third. At the end of the three years, he had saved from this, one hundred pounds, or five hundred dollars.

What did he do with it? The investment which he made of his thirty pounds, and of his fifteen shillings, you readily remember. They were put in the bank of family affection. And this went the same way. His brother Henry had engaged in a banking speculation, which proved to be a failure. His credit and property were in danger. Samuel went to him and begged him to accept his one hundred pounds; which he did, and which relieved him of his difficulties. The young man's care and love for his family were very great; doing for them was like doing for himself.

At the close of the three years, Henry took him into partnership, and this opened a wider scope to his powers. Already the business had thriven through his insight and energy; and more immediately under his control, it was destined to increase more and more. It was one of his favorite maxims, that "business is what it is made to be;" good, bad, indifferent, honest, or dishonest—just what it is made to be by the master-mind which conducts it.

The first great principle on which business was conducted by the Budgetts was cash payments. Do you know what that is? Goods were not bought or sold on credit. Articles were not *charged on the books*, to be paid for at some future time—often very future. They were paid for *at the time* of buying, in cash, or at least at a given time not many weeks or days off. In this way they avoided many "bad debts;" that is, losses from customers who, after three, or four, or six months, might find themselves in no situation to pay at all. The consequence of this system is, that merchants and traders know, with some degree of certainty, just where they are, in almost every stage of their business.

The store began small, and gradually enlarged. When Samuel first entered it, it was only a small retail shop. A great many of the customers were women, who came from the neighboring villages on donkeys; and oftentimes a great crowd of donkeys testified how many customers there were on hand, making a smart day's business behind the counters. Samuel thought, why not go around into the villages, and get the orders of their customers; it would save them trouble, it would secure their custom, and it would open ways to extend business. When Samuel joined the firm, he proposed this. Henry objected; he liked the old way of doing things. Samuel, however, prevailed over him, and gained his point; and soon he might have been seen setting off alone at stated times, going the rounds of the little villages in the vicinity, Pucklechurch and Doynton, and I do not know how many others, to meet his customers and get their orders for goods; his kind cheerful manners won upon every body who saw him, and he made friends wherever he went. From supplying families, he soon talked of supplying goods to the smaller shops. "It would be a great benefit to us," said the small shop-keepers. But Henry interfered. "Don't let us think of going into the wholesale trade," he said; "let us stick to the old course."

"We can but try a little extension in a small way," urged Samuel; "there is no risk." Henry was again obliged to give way, for there was no resisting a mind so ardent and resolute as Samuel's. And before long, the Budgetts supplied groceries to a large number of little shops dotting the country round; for England, you know, is more thickly settled than this country is, and there was a large population in and around Bristol.

An opportunity soon opened for further extension. And it is the work of a sagacious mind to *perceive* these opportunities when they occur, and to take advantage of them. It is this which promises success to the merchant.

The firm bought a large quantity of butter very cheap; in a few days, a rise in the price of butter took place in the market. "I will take this occasion," said Samuel, "to visit some of the large stores and offer to trade, for in this case it will evidently be for their advantage to buy." With him to purpose was to act, and therefore he undertook a journey into some of the large towns; but when it came to the point, he felt a little hesitation about facing men more largely engaged in trade. He however soon dashed that away; but he encountered, as he feared, many rudenesses and rebuffs. "Where are you from?" asked a man, in reply to his offers of the butter. "Kingswood," answered Samuel. "Kingswood!" cried the man scornfully; "you had better go back to Kingswood and mind your shop, and not try to sell *us* goods at Frome." Kingswood, you know, had a poor reputation, and people were slow to believe any good thing could come out of Kingswood. These rebuffs did not discourage the young man—not they. Besides, he succeeded in getting a few orders for his butter, for there were sensible men found who were willing to lay aside their pride, and candidly to acknowledge it was for their advantage to buy even from a shop at Kingswood. In a month he went around again, visited the same stores, met with pretty much the same sort of treatment, served faithfully his few customers, and perhaps got one or two more. Little by little he gained upon the prejudices of the people. Nothing damped him. "Try, try again," was his motto. "No gains without pains."

Never a single customer was neglected. The humblest was served with the same promptness and attention as the largest. With such resolution and energy, no wonder that business grew surprisingly, and that the foundation of a wholesale trade was laid on a firm footing. People began to stare, and look astonished. "What are the Budgetts about?" they said; and what was still more remarkable, they thought every body that dealt with them seemed to thrive also, for I suppose the firm breathed its own energy into every body that came in contact with it. That is the great advantage of being connected with men of thorough business habits; you get their habits. Of Samuel's perseverance you have had good proof; now let us glance at his notions of HONESTY.

At the time he began business, pepper in England lay under a heavy tax. In consequence of it, pepper was commonly adulterated; in almost every grocery store there might be seen a cask labelled P. D., (pepper dust,) filled with dust resembling pepper, with which real pepper was mixed before it was sold ; of course, a very much adulterated article. It had grown into a custom of the trade, and men regarded honest did it without stopping to think, or to question the principle which it involved.

A cask with P. D. marked on it was also found in Henry Budgett's store. As soon as Samuel had a responsibility in the store, his conscience began to grumble. That "every body did so," was an argument of no weight with him. If every body *did wrong*, it became him, then, to do right. It was "only a trick of the trade." But he did not believe in a trade that *had* tricks, or that could *stoop* to tricks, in order to live. The more he thought of it, the more he hated the sight of that ugly cask. It was neither more or less than a hypocrite, and he liked genuine things, goods or men. Besides, he was very sure he could not dare ask the *blessing of God upon the use it was put to,* and *this* decided him. He resolved instantly to act. It was night. He went into the store, rolled out the cask down to the old quarry where he used, when a boy, to pass a portion of his Sabbaths, and there he stove it in, and scattered the

P. D. to the four winds.   His conscience was clear.   After he got home and was in bed, he remembered the staves; there was no need of wasting them, he thought; and the first thing the next morning he went to the quarry, gathered them up, and put them aside for a better use.

This is what Christian principle does.   It is often said, there is more or less deception in trade, and that few articles are genuine where there can be clever cheating.   .We should be very sorry to believe this, or to suppose that success in business must in any way depend upon deception; or that the many Christian men engaged in trade would for one moment lend themselves to underhand dealings, or to any practices that would shun the daylight of common honesty.

On another occasion, a man professing to be a Christian came to Samuel one day, offering to tell him a secret which would put him in the way of making a good deal of money.   Upon what conditions the secret was disclosed, I do not know; but it proved to be a receipt for making sham vinegar at a very slight cost.

" What," cried Samuel Budget, when he fairly

found out what it was, "do you want to lead me into a dealing like this? If you are resolved to go to hell yourself, why should you try to drag me with you?"

The man found himself at the wrong counter to peddle sham wares. And the young merchant's honest indignation he did not probably soon forget. Indeed, he believed there was a right way to do almost every thing.

See what principle he infused into, and what a value he put upon a virtue too much neglected, if not quite despised, in these days, but a virtue of *great price*, the virtue of ECONOMY.

Passing through a chamber in one of his warehouses one day, where a new hand was at work cutting out paper bags to be used in the shop, he immediately saw that the boy did not do his work in the best manner, for he *wasted* both time and paper. He stopped and kindly showed the lad *how*—how to improve—how to make *paper bags right*, cutting out several bags himself, and pointing out the economy to be used in the use of the material, for even paper was not to be wasted.

"Of course," he said to the youth, "it would

be wronging *me* for you to continue to make the bags your way, and I suppose you would not wish to injure your employer, even in so small a thing as this. But think for a moment of the injury you would be doing to *yourself* if, when you have a business of your own, you have not learned how to manage it with economy; and you must take your first lessons in economy in things of this kind."

Even an old nail had its value. Two or three boys were kept in the establishment, after it became large, whose sole business was to pick up and hammer out old nails. This was the first thing a boy was set to do. If he hammered out old nails *well*, he was put to mend bags under the master bag-mender; this was his first step in promotion: if he mended bags well, he was promoted to be a messenger; and so he rises from step to step, according to his ability and industry. But the *foundation* of promotion and success is laid in doing the best you can at the anvil, or on the old bags.

Little things were never for one moment to be neglected because they were little. Boys, as clerks or in work-shops, often grumble at the small and insignificant things which they at first are often employed about. They do not know that these are *tests* of their ability and disposition to work. They do not know how much depends upon doing these *well—taking pains* to do them well. And many a boy has left a good place from a false notion that he was not doing much, because his tasks were humble; forgetting that fidelity to *these* was the only sure stepping-stone to higher duties. Let boys try always to remember that little habits, like all little things, more than make up by *their number* what they seem to lack in individual importance. They are the true seeds of character. We might as well plant acorns and not expect them to grow, as cherish small vices and bad habits, and not expect them to increase; or as reasonably expect to see the fine and noble oak where no acorns were planted, as true greatness and success in life where the seedlings of a thousand habits of industry and virtue had not been first carefully cultivated.

PUNCTUALITY was another of these little habits to which Samuel Budgett attached great importance in all the great and small affairs of life. And punctual himself, he took pains to make his clerks and workmen so. As business

increased, a large number of persons were employed. "When I first knew the business," said
an old man, "it had only five men and three
horses; now, three hundred men and one hundred horses are no more than enough." And
all these he was anxious to *educate* into 'that
measure of promptness and efficiency which
would make their services of value. His own
example must have been powerful. But I
suppose he found something more was necessary to stimulate dull minds and quicken lag-
ging feet, and he accordingly adopted a plan,
which Mr. Arthur thus describes. "At six
o'clock work began. By the side of the gate
which admitted the men into the wide enclo-
sure where business was transacted, hung a
black-board divided into squares; each square
was numbered and contained a nail, and on
this nail hung a little copper plate. Each man
had his number, and as he went out for the
night, he took his plate with him, leaving of
course his number exposed on the board. As he
entered he hung the plate on his nail, so covering
his number. The moment the bell ceased ringing—for there was a bell for business hours—
the board was taken down, and all whose num-

bers were not covered were marked defaulters. Those whose names were not found on the list of defaulters at the end of the year, were handsomely rewarded." The men liked it; it braced them up, and although many came three or four miles, they made it a point to be in season.

Mr. Budgett never allowed himself to be a minute late in keeping his engagements; he felt he had no right to steal others' time: and if any thing providentially did hinder him on the way, he made sincere apologies, even to a child.

With all this punctuality came DISPATCH. During the busy season, after their business had greatly increased, the men were often kept at work until ten or eleven o'clock at night. This greatly troubled Mr. Samuel Budgett; he could not bear to have it so.

"The men ought to be at home with their families," he would say; "they ought not to be here." By rearranging matters, the bell to leave off work was rung at half past eight. But this did not long satisfy him. "I do not like to see you here," he would say; "you must be at home evenings; you must have time for reading; you must have opportunity to take care of your souls; we must *get done* sooner here."

He then fixed upon seven o'clock to leave: *that*, people said, was impossible; business could not be finished. But that which was best and right to do, Mr. Budgett thought *could be* done. He did not stick at small difficulties, or create impossibilities out of mere difficulties. He meant to do right by his men, whether or no. He finally·pitched upon six o'clock as the regular hour to quit work. And such was the energy, method, and dispatch infused into every department of labor throughout this great warehouse, one hundred and eighty feet long, by three hundred and fifty feet at its greatest depth, that six o'clock found the clerks, salesmen, porters, wagoners, coopers, and I do not know how many others, with their day's work done, and *well done*. As you pass from loft to loft, office to office, yard to yard, visit the stables where forty or fifty horses are stabled, the carpenter's shop, the cooper's shop, you perhaps wonder how they ever get through. What multitudes of cheeses; how many tierces of sugar; then the bags of coffee, heaps of canary-seed, chests of tea, flour-barrels and flour-bags, raisins, etc. The Budgetts were "general produce merchants," and you can guess the variety and the quantity of things housed under their ample roof.

"But are not the men hurried and flurried?" Nothing was more remarkable about this gigantic hive, than the "marvellous order" which everywhere prevailed. There was no confusion, no clashing. And it was very evident that every body, from the boy who was picking up crooked nails to the soberest clerk at his desk, felt each that he had a responsible work to do; and that it was his interest and happiness, no less than his duty, to do it well.

Well-doing had its reward. Mr. Budgett knew the characters of the men in his employment. He made their characteristics and habits a study. He sympathized with them, invited their confidence, counselled them, visited their families, and showed them that he was not only or merely the head of affairs, but their *friend,* and *their* best interests he wished to further as well as his own.

One of his men said he would get twice as much out of them as any other master. How; by overworking them? We have seen that was not the way, but by teaching them how to work skilfully; by an honest sympathy with, and a hearty appreciation of their labors, and by rewarding them according to their diligence and improvement.

"Remember the gothic door," was sometimes whispered into the ear of an idler—if idlers were indeed allowed a place there, which may be doubted—at any rate, into the ear of any showing a disposition to shirk or lag.

"Remember the gothic door." What did this mean? The gate, I suppose, through which the men passed out at night, was of a gothic form; for here Mr. Budgett was often found standing on Friday night, his pocket looking very portly, and a basket in hand filled with small packages. As the men passed him, he gave a parcel to one and to another, which on being opened when they got home, were found to contain five shillings, or three shillings, or a crown, or half a crown, or something to show his estimate of their industry and faithfulness. Nor were the boys forgotten. They also received their pennies, as few or many as their diligence deserved; for the deserving were never overlooked.

"He never had a good year, but I was the better for it when stock-taking came," said one.

"At stock-taking he has sometimes given me a hundred pounds," said another who had been long in his service, after relating the pains Mr. Budgett had taken to make him what he was.

"He was a man as had no pleasure in muckin up money," adds another. "Why, he would often in that way give, aye, I believe, twenty pounds on a Friday night—well, at any rate, fifteen."

To his clerks and other men in the employment, he would often reply, "*My* business? It is not *my* business, but *ours*." He wanted every body to feel a joint interest in the concern, an affectionate participation in all its fortunes.

After stock-taking, which began at twelve o'clock on a certain day, and was all finished up long before twelve at night, a supper was usually given to the men, besides on other occasions when they were gathered together for social enjoyment and recreation. Here is a short notice of one of these occasions, taken from a Bristol paper, which will give you some idea of what they were. You will see it was after Mr. Budgett had been long in business, and after his store had been removed from Kingswood to Bristol, the occasion of which I shall relate to you. His home always remained at Kingswood.

"On Friday last," says the newspaper, "the neighborhood of Nelson-street was enlivened by a gay and busy movement in the establishment of Messrs. Budgett. The annual festival given to their men was on this occasion provided for them at the country residence of one of the partners, Samuel Budgett, Esq., of Kingswood Hill. Coaches, omnibuses, and carriages of nearly every description, were put in requisition to carry the inmates of this hive of industry to the spot. Ample preparation was there found for the recreation both of the body and the mind. At two o'clock, about two hundred of their business staff sat down to a sumptuous dinner in the open air on the lawn near the house, where the 'good cheer' found a cordial welcome and a hearty dispatch. This being ended, the party was soon joined by their wives and friends, to spend with each other the remainder of the day. There were athletic exercises, games, and a band of music. The pleasure-grounds, fruit-garden, and shrubberies were all thrown open to the company, and never was there a scene of greater enjoyment and social union. In the evening were three or four hundred assembled for tea under a large covered building, after which some animated speeches were delivered by the gentlemen present, among whom were the clergy and ministers of each denomination in the village.

"The day closed only too quickly, and we cannot do better than recommend a similar experiment to all who wish to cherish in their business one common feeling of interest, which ought always to exist between employers and the employed."

Among the evergreens used to decorate these occasions, we pick out some capital mottoes. Let us keep a few of them. "Perseverance surmounts difficulties." "May poverty be always a day's march behind us." "The blessing of the Lord maketh rich." "In all labor there is profit." "Whatsoever thy hand findeth to do, do it with all thy might." "Diligent in business, fervent in spirit."

But we must penetrate a little further into Mr. Budgett's character, and into the more secret places of this great establishment. There is one more habit to be spoken of—a habit, I am afraid, seldom found in places of business.

It is one which gives a hidden power to all other good habits, increasing their excellency, tempering their edge, and directing them as means to a great and wise end. It is the habit of daily prayer.

Every year, as soon as the brothers had taken their account of stock and struck the balance, they retired to an inner office, and kneeling down before God, acknowledged his hand in all the allotments of his providence, accepting success with gratitude, and disappointment and failure with humble submission to his holy will.

"I well remember," said a gentleman, "how grateful to my own heart was the discovery that every youth in that establishment had his own private sleeping-room, with the express understanding that this arrangement was made in order that he might feel himself alone with his Father which is in heaven, when at suitable times he might wish to retire to read his Bible, meditate, and pray."

"A habit of daily prayer," Mr. Arthur tells us, "existed in the concern from the beginning. When the business was only retail, all were gathered together as a family; and when it branched out, a portion of the premises at

Kingswood was set apart as a 'chapel,' and still stands there, serving many sacred purposes. After their removal to Nelson-street, in Bristol, this admirable habit was maintained, and a room was devoted to this purpose. One of those who knew every joint of the establishment, who had risen with it, and loved it as his own, remarked how this practice tended to make the men orderly and regular in their ways, even where decided piety was not known. 'Besides, sir,' said the man, 'in this way the men get to pray for the blessing of God on the business, and there is a great deal in that. Many would like to be as we are, but they cannot without the same blessing.'"

In a religious paper of 1847, we find the following interesting article :

"EXAMPLE TO MERCANTILE ESTABLISH-
MENTS.

"'Not slothful in business; fervent in spirit.'

"On the second of November, after a drive of several miles from the country, at half-past seven in the morning, I dropped unintentionally into the extensive and long warehouses of the Messrs. Budgett, in Nelson-street. I heard singing, the 'voice of rejoicing and salvation,' in one of the upper rooms. The senior clerk said to me, 'Our men are engaged in morning prayers; will you not step up? Do, sir.' I did so, and entered a room thirty or forty feet long, furnished with benches having comfortable backs, closely placed; and at the upper end was a table and large fire. I was surprised and delighted to find from fifty to one hundred, for every seat was occupied, chiefly porters in their white frocks, all sitting in the stillness and seriousness of family devotion. At the table sat an interesting, devout laborer, giving out one of our beautiful hymns with a tenderness and pathos which touched my heart. After singing, I was requested to lead their devotions. The Bible lay open on the table at the twenty-fifth chapter of Matthew. I read the appropriate parables of the virgins and the talents. We then fell on our knees and worshipped the God of all commerce in earth or seas, when every man arose to attend the call of active duty. I felt it no common privilege to join with those praying porters and devout clerks; and the scene, so good, and coming so unexpectedly, has left an impression upon me which I shall not soon forget. Is not this an example to all commercial establishments—an example worthy of general imitation? Here is a noble room for the daily worship of God in the heart of a range of warehouses, and the large number of hands employed therein have a regular portion of time allotted to them for that holy purpose. Precision, order, energy, and exactness, are principles engraved on every department of the vast business conducted here. But every thing is 'sanctified by the word of God and prayer;' and therefore it is no matter of surprise to those who have faith in the Bible, that the proprietor of this exemplary mercantile establishment, in addition to his having much peace and piety among his men, has risen from low and small beginnings to great wealth and prosperity. 'Him that honoreth me, I will honor.'

"A WESLEYAN MINISTER."

CHAPTER IV.

HIDDEN LIFE—FIRE—THE CHILDREN—DOING GOOD.

You will perhaps like to leave business and follow Mr. Budgett home, or go with him by the way, and observe him in his daily paths. Soon after he entered into partnership with Henry, he married a worthy young woman, and took a little cottage in a lane opposite the shop. Was he mainly bent on getting ahead in the world? Did his business chiefly occupy him? Let us see. A little record was found, which discloses his inward thought at this interesting period, when the young couple were beginning the journey of life together. It is dated Jan. 24, 1822.

" *Resolved,* 1. To seek a deeper sense and clearer discovery of my awful state through sin.

" 2. To seek to get satisfactory evidence that I am accepted through Christ.

" 3. To make the service of God, and obedience to the dictates of his Spirit, the supreme object of my life.

" 4. To begin to redeem time; to be more

moderate in my eating, drinking, and sleeping, and to endeavor to make one word pass for two, in order that *my soul may grow in grace* and be happy ; and all this I would do in humble dependence on the continual help of the Holy Spirit.

" 5. To read every day a chapter or two of Scripture."

Let every one read and ponder these. The young merchant set apart seasons for rigid self-examination. He remembered there was a Judge on high who was an exact, though not a hard master, to whom the thoughts and the intents of the heart are known.

The following account with himself was found in pencil among his papers, dated a few years after the last.

"Sunday Evening, Aug. 3, 1823.

1. I am conscious I have thought of myself more highly than I ought to think.

" 2. I have sacrificed to my own net, and burnt incense to my own drag.

" 3: I have ascribed my success to my own wisdom.

" 4. I have boasted of what I have received as if I had not received it.

" 5. I have gloried in very many things, save the cross of our Lord Jesus Christ.

" 6. I have desired the praise of man, and taken pleasure in it.

" 7. I have repeatedly given way to foolish desires.

" 10. I have often allowed myself to speak, if not lies, yet what was not, in the strict sense, truth in the love thereof.

- " 12. I have not labored to do whatsoever I did to the glory of God.

" 13. I have indulged my bodily appetites."

You see how strict and searching he was with himself. Secret sins, lurking within the soul, he hunted out, brought to light, and was greatly oppressed on account of them.

"I shall never be happy," he says, "until I find a Saviour from the love, the power, the guilt, and the sad effects of sin. I believe such a Saviour is provided, but he is not my Saviour; yet I am resolved to try if I cannot find him. I will seek him first and oftenest, and with the utmost diligence, for I am in danger till I do find him."

With all the prosperity which began to roll in upon the firm after Samuel joined it, he did not neglect to make the prosperity of his soul of *chief* account.   He never lost sight of his treasure in heaven, or forgot that it was of far higher value than any earthly riches.

"AN ALARMING FIRE."

Under this head what do we find? "About half-past seven on Tuesday evening," what year I do not know, "great alarm was felt throughout Bristol by the appearance upon the horizon of a fire, evidently of immense extent, the heavens being completely lit up with it, at about five or six miles distant.   Large crowds of people immediately congregated upon Kingsdown and the various hills, and conjecture was rife as to where it was raging.   The arrival of an express messenger on horseback for engines and firemen, brought the news that the conflagration was upon the premises of Messrs. H. H. & S. Budgett, at Kingswood Hill.   The Messrs. Budgett are among the most extensive flour, sugar, tea, and general merchants in this part of the kingdom, and are well known throughout England for their extensive mercantile transactions.   They have several establishments in Bristol, but for reasons unknown to us, have always held their central establishment at Kingswood Hill. The fire was discovered by one of their men, at about quarter past seven, in a room called the titler-room, in which refined sugars are kept; and it is supposed originated in one of the flues communicating to that room. A messenger was instantly sent to Bristol; and in the mean time the alarm spread rapidly through the village and neighborhood, all the inhabitants of which immediately went to assist in subduing the fire. Their efforts, it was hoped at first, would have been successful; but in a few minutes the fire spread in a most alarming manner, and speedily communicated with the entire range of warehouses. At this period the Norwich Union engines arrived and played on the fire; the engines of the other offices also speedily arrived. The fire in the warehouses had, however, now reached so great a height that it was evident their total destruction was inevitable; and the efforts of all, therefore, were directed to saving the adjoining dwelling-houses, upon which the engines played, to cut off communication with the burning warehouses. These efforts were happily successful, and both the dwelling-houses and the

stables of the establishment, in which were
forty-seven valuable horses, were saved. The
fire in the warehouses continued raging till four
o'clock in the morning, when it was got under;
but not until all the warehouses, the counting-
rooms, and the retail shop had been completely
destroyed. The books, however, were saved.
This was most fortunate, as their loss to a house
of such transactions as the Messrs. Budgett
would have been irretrievable. The stock consumed consisted of refined sugars, cheese, coffee,
teas, flour, and must have amounted to several
thousands. They had just imported two large
cargoes of fruit, and a heavy stock of sugars,
which were, however, in their Bristol warehouses. The firm were insured to a large
amount—eight thousand pounds in the Phenix,
and other sums in various offices."

Beyond the sums insured, their pecuniary loss
was about fifteen thousand dollars; a heavy and
unexpected check to the rising merchants. All
earthly goods may perish in a few hours. The
evening sun may set on our thrift and comfort
and goodly possessions; the morning sun may
rise on their smoking ruins. These pious merchants, no doubt, accepted the disaster as the

wise ordering of His providence who doeth all things well, and they set about immediately to repair the breach thus suddenly and fearfully made in their business.

What was to be done? A circular was issued and sent to all their customers in the morning, stating the impossibility of fulfilling their orders for that day, but on the *next day* the goods should be sent as usual. Mr. Budgett hastened to Bristol, hired a building next to a small warehouse which he already had in that city, set every body to work, organized his business, was in readiness to dispatch his goods according to promise, and henceforth made Bristol the seat of the firm, where it grew and enlarged and prospered, and was perfected into that remarkable system which made it a model mercantile concern, worthy both of scrutiny and imitation.

In progress of time Mr. Budgett bought the old quarry hallowed by the Sabbath memories of his boyhood, filled it up, and made it into a beautiful garden. The little cottage in the lane was in time exchanged for a large and substantial dwelling-house, surrounded by green lawns, hedge-rows, fruit-trees, and shade-trees, in the planting and growth of which he took great delight. All the beauties of the outward world he had an eye to see and a heart to enjoy.

" Can you help admiring the present beautiful weather?" he says. "See how spring and summer are approaching already. The birds sing merrily; the days lengthen fast; the flowers are beginning to decorate the hedges and the banks; the fields are increasing in verdure and beauty; and I hope you and I shall endeavor to keep pace with all nature in praising our Creator and Redeemer."

His excellent mother lived to see the prosperity and usefulness of her beloved son. The last we hear of her is from a letter written by Samuel to his sister in January, 1831.

"I have just returned from Winterbourn," he writes, "from beholding one of the most interesting sights this world affords; I mean the happy, truly happy, sick and dying bed of a saint ripe for glory. Such is our dear mother. You have seen her. She is not now less happy, only less sensible of her pain. Her soul still triumphs in prospect of the glory which awaits her, and which in all probability she will in a few days be introduced to.

"'Mark the perfect man,' etc. How is that text illustrated in her experience! 'May it be equally so in yours and mine. In order to that, we have to *live the life* of the righteous, and we are sure to die the death. I hope, my dear sister, you are making progress. Remember, we are safe and happy only as we are vigorously pressing forward. To halt is to go back."

But as the old friends and beloved relatives of a past generation dropped into their graves, a new and young generation was springing up around him. Sons and daughters were born to him; nephews and nieces gladdened him by their visits; young people loved to seek his counsel and share in his affections.

Home he endeavored to make a happy place for his children—a place where they loved best to be, and where every innocent amusement was provided for play hours and healthful recreation. There we find donkeys to ride, chickens to rear, rabbits, guinea-pigs, dogs; garden beds to cultivate, gooseberries and currant-bushes to look after, swings, etc. Mr. Budgett loved to be with his children; he sympathized with them in all their joys and sorrows, and very early invited their sympathy with him.

He used to talk with them about his business and daily affairs, explain to them his reasons for pursuing this or that course of action, ask their advice, disclose his perplexities, and thus teach them to think and to judge and feel upon important matters at an age when most parents would banish their children from the family councils to the school-room or the playground.

He believed that children were *entitled to the society of their parents;* that it was one mode, and one important mode of educating them in the knowledge, the duties, and obligations of practical life. Parents perhaps sometimes overlook this, and leave their children to gain their knowledge of the world from intercourse which they could the least desire.

But the *one* great aim, the one constant prayer for his children, was their conversion to God. Less than that gave no satisfaction to his soul. They were surrounded by every influence favorable to Christian nurture—the family altar, the sacred keeping of the Sabbath, godly acquaintance, works of Christian charity, sympathy with every good thing; and yet this pious father felt that something more was necessary to renew and sanctify the heart—the influence

of the Holy Spirit.   He was instant in season
and out of season in parental faithfulness to
bring them tó a like precious faith in Christ,
which was the sun and the joy of his own soul.
The following letter shows the tender concern
of a pious father's heart.

"MY DEAR SARAH·ANN—Your kind note I
duly received by the hand of your brother
James, for which I thank you.   Be assured that
it gives me much pleasure to know that I am
affectionately remembered by any member of
my family, and especially by our little daugh-
ter.   I hope you are trying to be a good girl.
If you knew how much the happiness of those
who love you depended on your conduct, I think
that if nothing else proved a sufficient motive
to good behavior, that would ; but then my
dear little girl knows very well that her own
happiness, both in this world and the next, depends upon her giving her heart to God.   Do
not, my dear child, live one hour without being
satisfied that God is just now pleased with you,
that is, that you have his favor ; for we are
happy if we share his smile, his counsel, and
his care.   May you, my child, be truly devoted

to God in youth, and then you will be prepared for a useful life, or for early death. You may write me as often as you please, and I will try to answer your letters. Tell me all the workings of your little mind, all your hopes and all your fears, all your joys and all your sorrows."

And this faithful and praying parent did have the happiness of seeing his children, one by one, early in life become penitent believers in Christ; walking in the path of his commandments, growing in the knowledge of God, and with "ready mind and active will" fulfilling the duties of the Christian life. Few parents can write as here follows :

"MY DEAR LITTLE SALLY—Your kind letter to mamma we duly received, and I should have written to you before now, but I have been very unwell, so weak that I have scarcely been able to read or write; but I am thankful to inform you I am now getting better, and I hope soon to recover my strength. I assure you, we think and talk of you very often, and we do not cease to pray for you. What a mercy it is, my dear child, that as a family we are all seeking our happiness from one source, and that the right one. How insignificant does every thing else look when compared with this, even in this life, and in the possession of health, wealth, and all that the world calls great and good ; but look a little further—a sick-bed, a dying hour, a judgment-day, all of which will very soon be present ; and how then shall we value all besides this one thing needful, this divine love! The Lord fill my dear child's *heart ;* and then from the abundance of the heart the mouth will speak, and you will, you *must,* however unconsciously, be made useful to others.

> 'Tis worth living for this,
> To administer bliss,
> And salvation in Jesus' name. -

I believe we are all as a family going to heaven. Glory be to God.

> " Yours, affectionately,
> "PAPA AND MAMMA."

What a fountain of holy joy does this letter disclose within this Christian household. His success, his prosperity, his worldly connections, his houses and his lands, all sink in value before the higher blessing of a whole family converted to Christ, members of the household of faith. "*He* blesseth the habitation of the just." The happiness of how many prosperous families is imbittered by the waywardness, the danger, the ruin of a son ; the comfort of how many pious parents is destroyed by the irreligion and free-thinking of their children. Why is this ? Is there any such defect or failure in parental discipline or watchfulness as may serve as a warning and corrective to the anxious and perplexed spirits of thousands of other parents seeking to bring up their children in the nurture and admonition of the Lord?

Mr. Budgett early gave his sons responsible posts in his business; and as a proof of the confidence which he placed in them, when the oldest of his boys was but twenty-one, he allowed the four to take a journey on the continent by themselves, with no confidential servant or faithful friend to watch over their goings; nor was the confidence misplaced or abused ; their virtues seemed strengthened by the very expectations which they well understood their father had of them.

The busy merchant and faithful father also found time to encourage and quicken the hearts of other youth besides those more immediately related to him by kindred or business.

"We cannot indeed too highly value time," he writes to a young friend. "In this I have been truly deficient. If we would rise early, we must begin at the right end, that is, by going to bed early, or all will be lost labor. You must have seven hours sleep. An alarum is a very good thing; but if we neglect the call a few times, like the calls of the Spirit on our consciences, it will be ineffectual.

"I am glad you still retain love to God after seven years' experience. May it be increased seven times seven. I think nothing is so calculated to remove reserve as zeal for God and humility. We think too much of ourselves, and not enough of the importance of being found faithful. May you, my dear friend, become truly simple of heart, and dead to the opinion of others when it stands in the way of duty. You have not wearied me. Your letters are no tax on my time. I am always very glad to hear from you, and the more freely you write to me, the more you please me."

On another occasion we find him thus writing to a young Sabbath-school teacher.

"My very dear Friend—I am truly thankful that God has so graciously inclined your heart to seek your happiness where alone true enjoyment can be found, and that He has not only blessed, but made you a blessing.

"If you are faithful, He will give you grace to lose yourself in him, as a drop in the ocean, and your prayers will be frequently offered and graciously answered.

> "'Keep me dead to all below,
> Only Christ resolved to know,
> Firm and disengaged and free,
> Seeking all my bliss in thee.'

"You will feel so impressed with the value of souls and your responsibility to God, that you will never rest until all the girls in your class are brought from darkness to light. I remember a young person who had thirteen scholars, and for several years she saw but little fruit of her labor, until she was almost discouraged; but instead of giving up, she began to wrestle with God in earnest, persevering, faithful prayer; and in a short time one of the girls showed a serious concern for her spiritual welfare, and began to inquire with deep anxiety what she must do to be saved. This soon

spread through the class, and in a few months
every child gave satisfactory evidence that her
heart was changed."

One favorite mode of doing good was the time-
ly lending of religious books and tracts. Christian biography he regarded as choice reading,
as tending to quicken growth in grace, and urge
us on in the divine life.

"But all good things require to be read pray-
erfully, and in faith," he says. "And are we
not too apt to think there was something pecul-
iar in the *individuals*, rather than in the *faith* by
which they derived all their excellences? The
fountain of all good is as full and as free of ac-
cess *now*, and *to us*, as ever it was to them; and
we have only to exercise the same faith, and all
the good will be as surely ours as ever it was
theirs."

Thus he extracted good where others perhaps only sought enjoyment. "No gains without pains," in self-knowledge or religious improvement.

He seldom went out to walk, or for a drive,
without a bundle of tracts or a pocketful of
little books. And one room in his house was
indeed a sort of Tract and Sabbath-school book

depository, lined with shelves, where he kept a large stock on hand for distribution. It was seldom lean or empty, for he was in the habit of replenishing it every now and then by fifty dollars' worth of reading at a time.

"With respect to his liberality to the cause of God, he far excelled any one that *I* ever met with in the church of Christ," said a clergyman who knew him well ; and this we can readily believe.

When an application was made to him for any benevolent object, he never was heard to excuse himself, either wholly or in part, from it, by saying, "I have had *so many* cases lately," though many he must have had.

If asked by any one who knew all the circumstances of the case for which his charity was needed, his reply often was, "Well, how much do you think I ought to give?" And whether it was five, ten, fifteen, or twenty pounds, the sum was cheerfully given. Many a bank-note and sovereign did he leave at the parsonage, or slip into his minister's hand, to be distributed as he thought necessary among the poor of his flock. Nor did he confine these benefactions to his own pastor ; the other clergymen of his neighborhood were often the stewards of his bounty.

To give you another instance of his readiness to do good, and his ability in carrying out
his plans, I will abbreviate a little story told
by Mr. Arthur. One Sunday evening, on Mr.
Budgett's return from a neighboring village,
where he had been exhorting in an evening
lecture, he passed squads of rough-looking, idle,
lawless lads lounging on the grass, but jogging
on to ruin. He stopped and began to talk with
them, and talked until he secured their attention. "Now," said he at ending, "if I gave
you a good tea, would you like to come and
take it?"

"Oh yes, oh, yes!" the boys answered. It
was what, I fancy, they seldom had.

"Come, then," said Mr. Budgett in his friendly tone, "to the vestry of Kingswood chapel
to-morrow evening. We are going to have a
little meeting, and you shall have a good tea."

It was to be a tea-meeting for the tract dis-
tributers.

The boys came, tickets were handed them,
and they ate and drank as hungry boys who
seldom see so nicely set tables might be supposed to do. "And have you had a good supper?" asked Mr. Budgett.

" 'Ees, thank 'ee."

" I dare say you know many young men who go about in the lane Sunday night." .

" O 'ees."

" Do you think, if I promised them a good tea, they would like to come here ?"

The boys thought none of them would object to the tea; but they looked shy, and there was a " but" in the way. . Mr. Budgett did not stop to inquire what. it was; but a hundred tickets were soon made out, to be handed to their fellows, all the " Toms, Dicks, and Harrys" round about, inviting them to a bountiful treat at the chapel hall on Mr. Budgett's premises. A good many of them hesitated about accepting the invitation; "they did not want to.be hooked into a prayer-meeting," they said. However, there was the promised treat; they were sure they did not want to lose their chance at that; so, among the ringleaders, the matter was compromised in this way: they would go and take tea, and then "bolt" as soon as it was over, for they of. course concluded their host had some religious end to be answered, and " they had no mind to be done good to."

On the appointed evening every thing was

arranged; a hundred of them came, as wild, uncouth, and unpromising a set of guests as was ever gathered together. It was evident, after a while, that in one group seemed to be the " ringleaders ;" and the coarse and boisterous words which proceeded from it, seemed to defy any attempt to tame or to restrain them. But the good merchant and *his* party knew the stuff they had to deal with. Towards the close of the supper, one of Mr. Budgett's sons, James or Edwin, for both went heart and hand with their father in his labors of love, pushed into this group, and began a talk with the leader, a rough, sailor-like looking fellow, who first tried by his wit and rudeness to put the "young gentleman" down. It soon grew more evident that a preconcerted signal to go was near at hand, when Mr. Budgett went into the desk, and said, "I asked you to come here for the purpose of doing something for you—something that will be of use to you. Now, just as a start, I will give you fifty pounds, and you must make up your minds what you will do with it."

Fifty pounds! They could run away from a prayer-meeting, but to run away from fifty pounds was quite another sort of thing, and not to be thought of. Hats were off, feet were turned from the door, and all eyes turned to the desk.

"Fifty pounds!" exclaimed one of Mr. Budgett's friends, who understood what was his aim, and yet was around among his rough guests— "fifty pounds! that's something. Why, there are about a hundred of us; and suppose we divide it among us, there will be half a sovereign apiece."

A very agreeable plan to most of the company, no doubt, but very far from the reckoning of their host.

"No, no!" started up another friend of Mr. Budgett; "it would be very foolish to throw away fifty pounds in such a manner. Can't we put it to some use that will do us good, and make it last?" and so the matter came up for a spirited discussion *what use* to put the money to, which soon kindled a great interest even among the most stupid and depraved of the street youth. And the affair was so managed that it issued in a motion to form a society for mental improvement, to be called the "Kingswood Young Men's Association." The motion was seconded and carried by a strong vote. And when, in the final arrangement, several of these rough fellows were placed on committees to carry out their plans, it was curious to witness the surprise, interest, and gratification which lighted up their sharp, trickish-looking faces. Mr. Budgett was voted in treasurer, and their place of meeting was appointed at the vestry of the chapel, after the Sunday evening service. So far so good, and the party separated with mutual good-will.

But how many would be likely to reappear on the next Sabbath evening? Sixty came; and the number testified what encouragement there is to labor even in the most unpromising fields. Let Christian men and women go to work *just where they are*, in God's name, for the good of souls, and nothing will surprise them more than the *vanishing of discouragements*, and the tokens of hope and success which will cheer them on the way. "Whatsoever thy hand findeth to do, *do it* with thy might," and the moral heathenism of our villages and cities will shrink into a diminished compass, if not quite away, before the warm affections and redeeming power and living elements of the gospel of Jesus Christ.

That little verse contains the vital principle of the whole matter.

"The Association" regularly held meetings on Sunday night, and once a week for secular instruction. A library was bought with the fifty pounds, lectures were sometimes given by the masters of the Kingswood schools, and year by year a tea-meeting was given, at which books were sometimes given as rewards.

According to the great law of Christian benevolence, that the more it does the more it wants to do, this successful movement for the moral improvement of the young men, suggested to Mr. Budgett the importance and necessity of something similar for the young women. This was accordingly done. And once a year, also, the "Young Females' Association" met on his grounds, to enjoy a delicious supper on tea and strawberries. This, however, was but a little of the real good which they received during the year. These associations cost Mr. Budgett about two hundred dollars a year, and proved to be one of his sagacious and profitable investments, for it gave him the clear returns of numbers saved from vice, the moral and mental improvement of many, and conversions to God not a few. A Bible class he formed and took charge of among the young women, which was abundantly blessed of God, and which at the time of his death numbered forty.

On one occasion he said to a friend, "Every morning, before you leave your room, inquire, 'Lord, what wouldst thou have me to do?' and every evening ask yourself, 'How much owest thou unto thy Lord?' Keep *short reckonings with him*, go forward; and your path shall be as that of the just, shining more and more unto the perfect day."

Was not herein the secret spring of *his* labors?

CHAPTER V.

THE POOR—A SUDDEN STROKE—HAPPY
ENDING.

Mr. Budgett was emphatically the poor man's friend, and the poor always *felt* him to be their friend. In his intercourse with them, he never forgot the small courtesies of life. His friendliness they never doubted, and therefore reproof and counsel they received from him with respect and thankfulness, even when not followed by amendment. His words by the way, were more valuable than scatterings of gold.

The "hauliers" of the coal-carts running between Kingswood and Bristol, a rough and bullying set of fellows, often provoking quarrels with other travellers on the road, could never resist the pleasant "good-morning" of the pious merchant, or scarcely dare fire off their volley of oaths in his hearing, or show fight, if he were discovered in the distance.

One afternoon as he was driving a friend into Bristol, the road in one place was almost blocked up by the return wagons of the "hauliers," who had stopped and stepped in to a neighboring inn. A boy was sent in to call them out. "Why, is this you, B——?" cried Mr. Budgett, as a stout-built fellow with a face begrimed with coal, came bustling out of the house, drawing the back of his hand across his mouth, fresh from the can. "I am sorry to see *you* there; here, come round to me:" then lowering his voice, he said kindly, "B——, my poor fellow, you have a wife and children at home. Have they any thing to eat?" "Not much, I be afeared, sir," said the man, trying to smile, though looking much ashamed.

"Well, tell me now, how much have you just spent?" asked Mr. Budgett.

"Why, threepence; but I had it gee'd by th' lady 'at had t' coal."

"Well, never mind who gave it to you, but tell me what you spent when you went into Bristol this morning?"

"Why, threepence."

"Well, the lady did not give you that; but no matter how you came by the money, so it was honestly got. What I want you to think about is this: by your own showing, you have spent sixpence to-day on beer; if you have done

the same every day this week, then you have
three shillings less in your pocket than you
might have had. Now, as you go along, just
consider how many little things that three shillings would have bought for the real comfort of
your wife, yourself, and your children ; you say
you fear they have little to eat at home now,
and you have spent sixpence upon yourself"—
an English sixpence is twelve of our cents. "Is
that kind? Nay, don't make any excuses. I
know you feel you have done wrong. Don't,
my poor fellow, repeat it. One word more;
if you persist in this habit, you will become a
drunkard, and the Bible tells you, 'Drunkards
shall not inherit the kingdom of God.' It will
lead you into all wickedness, and the Bible tells
you, 'The wicked shall be turned into hell.'
B——," he added solemnly, "think of this;
tell your companions there what I have said to
you; and above all, pray that God may bless
what I have said to you, and that he may make
you a more thoughtful and better man."

. The poor man listened with respectful attention. His look became downcast. "Thank
you, sir," he said with much feeling when his
friend ceased speaking. "It is very good for

gentlemen such as you, to talk this way to poor men like me."

During the scarcity of bread, in 1846 and 1847, he employed one hundred and fifty extra hands on small wages; adding every Saturday night, to those who had families, what might be sufficient to meet their daily wants. Thousands he spent merely to give employment, for maintaining men in idleness he felt was a bounty without a blessing.

Not having leisure for visiting the poor as much as he desired, in order to ascertain their destitution, and what kind of help they stood in greatest need of, he hired a visitor in his stead, a neighbor, who labored in this good work, dropping the sympathies and the charities of the busy merchant into many a comfortless home and wretched bosom.

He noticed, at one time, an unusually downcast and sad expression on the face of one of his men. Finding it did not wear off, he sent for him to his counting-room, and after a while, drew from him the story of his secret burden. "Master, I am in debt," said the poor man in tones of grief, "and every time I go near the river something bids me fling myself into it,

telling me there's water enough to rid me of all
my troubles, and that if I don't I shall be sent
into the prison there for debt."

Upon farther inquiry, it was found to have
grown out of the long sickness of his wife, and
having assured himself that the man ·had not
broken the regulation of a Society of which he
was a member, "Not to contract a debt without at least a reasonable prospect of discharg-
ing it," Mr. Budgett asked him if the payment
of his debts would restore his peace of mind.
The man looked as if *that* could not be.

"Well, come," said the merchant, "I do not
think things are quite so bad as they appear to
be. See here, my poor fellow, you owe ——
pounds: it's a very large sum for a man like
you, to be sure; but if you had run into debt
to any thing like this amount through extrav-
agance or thoughtlessness, I should have regarded it as an act of dishonesty on your part,
and I might have felt it right to discharge you.
But you are to be pitied, and not to be blamed.
Cold pity alone goes for nothing, so let us see
how you can be helped out of your troubles.
Now, do you think your creditors, considering
all the circumstances, would take one·half, and

be satisfied? here is Dr. Edwards, his bill is the heaviest; if we can get him to take one half—"

"One half, master!" exclaimed the poor man; "but if they *would* take one half, where 's the money to come from? I ar'n't got a shilling in the world, but what 's coming to me Friday night; and when I take my wages now, I ar'n't any pleasure in looking at the money, because it ar'n't my own; it should go to pay my debts, and I 'm obliged to use it to buy victuals. I think I shall never be happy again."

Deeply affected by the poor man's case, Mr. Budgett begged him to cheer up, for a friend had placed in his hands a sum equal to one half of his debts; he then sent him back to his work, and on his way, to order his horse to be harnessed, and brought around to him in ten minutes. Mr. Budgett drove round to all the man's creditors, compromised with them, and brought home their bills receipted in full for the respective debts. The man was again sent for to the counting-room, and as bill after bill was handed to him, he could only clutch them with a stare of wonder and strange uncertainty.

"But, master," he at last cried, when words

came, "where's the money come from?" "Never
mind that," answered his master; "go home and
tell your wife you are out of debt, you are an
independent man. I only hope the creditors
have felt something of the satisfaction in forgiving you one half of your debt to them, that
we know God feels in forgiving our debts to
him for Christ's sake; I have said that much
to all of them."

"But, master, where's the money come from?"
asked the man, with a still puzzled and bewil-
dered look.

"Well, well, I told you a Friend had given
it to me for you. *You* know that Friend as
well as I do. There now, you may leave your
work for to-day; go home to your wife, and
thank that Friend together for making you an
independent man. But stay, I had almost forgotten one thing: I called to see Mr. P——
as I drove through Stoke's Croft. I told him
the errand that had taken me from home all
day, and he gave me a sovereign for you to
begin the world with."

It would perhaps be difficult to tell which
was the happiest, the master or his man.

"Bear ye one another's burdens, and *so* fulfil

the law of Christ." Is it a law we are suffi-
ciently mindful of? ⁻

And thus the current of Mr. Budgett's life
flowed on. Foes, ingratitude, disappointments,
crosses, he indeed met with, but they never discouraged him from good, they never daunted
him in conflicts with evils, they never dimmed
the sunshiny friendliness of his nature.

"No pains, no gains," contains within itself
the very elements of combat and of victory.
"No cross, no crown," is the condition of our
title to heaven.

But there may be some who would know
more of the inner life of this eminent servant
of God. Was he, so diligent in business, so
fervent in spirit, ever subject to darkness of
mind? Did the tempter ever hard besiege him?
Did a sense of shortcoming and unprofitable-
ness ever obscure his hope of heaven? Let him
answer for himself.

"KINGSWOOD HILL, Nov. 23, 1843.

"MY DEAR BROTHER JAMES—I forced my
heavenly Father to use the rod, but I am astonished to think with what gentleness he has cor-
rected me. The first Sunday I was unwell, I
made a fresh act of faith, and ventured my

whole soul on the atonement. My heart seemed
to have been broken in a thousand pieces, and
I felt like weeping my life away for having
grieved my God. For the first week I held
fast my confidence, and felt calm as in the
hands of my loving Saviour. But on the second
Sabbath I grew much worse, so that I had little
hope of recovery. I began to reason with the
enemy, and let go my shield of faith; and then
was truly the hour and the power of darkness.
I can never describe the bitter anguish I felt
on reviewing my past life, and great horror and
gloom came over my mind with the thoughts of
being but just saved as by the skin of my teeth,
or of appearing before my Maker as an unprofitable servant, or perhaps of being a wander-
ing spirit cast out from God for ever.

—"My agony of mind was such that I thought
I was dying, and really fainted away. I then
recovered, and then tried to recover my shield
of faith; but on Monday morning, Satan was
again permitted to buffet me, and the conflict
was extreme. My dear sister Elizabeth then
came to my assistance, and said I was doing very
wrong; that I ought to come to the Saviour as
at first I came, and that she believed I would

recover; but that if I died, I was safe for heaven. I immediately took courage, and said, 'Lord, I *did* believe, and was happy; and thou hast said, 'Him that cometh unto me I will in no wise cast out.' I come, I believe—I *will*, I *do* believe.' My heart seemed melted to tenderness, and the name of Jesus was exceedingly precious. Sister Elizabeth then said, 'Cannot you now put in your claim for the blessing of full salvation? Remember the promise, 'I will circumcise thy heart.'' I said, 'I am suffering all this, because I would not take the necessary pains to obtain that blessing, when that very promise was so often and so powerfully impressed on my mind; and it was so clearly my duty to obtain, to enjoy, and to preach that great and glorious gospel privilege to others. I could not hold fast even a sense of my acceptance with God, or overcome various temptations to sin, and it is of the Lord's mercies that I am not consumed;' but when sister Elizabeth said, 'Put in your claim *now*,' I cried, 'Lord, thou hast said, 'I will circumcise,' etc.; now fulfil thine own word; I hang upon thy word; thou wilt do it. I dare believe.' I did not struggle long before my heart seemed deeply humbled, filled with love unutterable to God and all mankind. I however, could not entertain an idea that God could spare my life; and though I felt safe and happy, I could not feel willing to die, even to go to heaven, with such a consciousness of unfaithfulness up to the eleventh hour, and earnestly prayed, 'Oh, *spare* me a little, that I may recover strength before I go hence, to be here no more.' On the following morning my dear wife came into my room with the Bible in her hand, saying, 'I have just opened upon this passage: 'For my name's sake will I defer mine anger, and for my praise will I refrain for thee, that I cut thee not off. Behold, I have refined thee, but not with silver; I have chosen thee in the furnace of affliction.' Isaiah 48 : 9, 10.' Never did Scripture so powerfully impress my mind. I said, 'It is the word of God to me,' in answer to his servant's prayers; I shall not die, but live.'

"From that time I never entertained a doubt but that I should have another opportunity of preaching salvation, full salvation by Jesus Christ, to every one who will put in their claim for it. My mind has since been kept in perfect peace, and I have been gradually recovering.

"Now, my dear brother James, my object in being thus minute in the description is, first to lead you, as you would avoid the gloom, the horror, the anguish, such as no tongue can tell, or the more tremendous consequences, of being hurried out of time into eternity; as you would enjoy this life tenfold more than you possibly can without it; as you would be unspeakably happy, safe, useful, and rising daily in refinement and elevation of character; and as you would have a glorious entrance administered to you among the saints in light: in a word, as you would escape hell, and gain heaven securely, that you at once give the Lord your *whole* heart, and accept his full salvation. This, my dear brother, is much easier than doing it by halves. I am, my dear brother, most affectionately, yours,   "S. B."

In Edwin the second son, appeared, more than in any other of the children, the marked traits of his father. In business, sagacity, decision, and promptness. At home, he was the obedient child, and loving brother; at the Sunday-school, a faithful teacher; in the prayer-meeting, "fervent, devout, and prevailing;"

among the poor, the sympathizing, active, personal friend and helper. His buoyant spirits, his joyous smile, his unaffected piety, his sweet song, made him a delightful companion to the young and the old. Never, perhaps, was there a more beautiful example of household religion than that in which he was reared, and no branch of the parent stock was more vigorous, more fruitful, more full of promise, than he. He was a young man whom the church could not afford to lose, and whom the world stood in need of.

Never perhaps, in this Christian family, was their cup more full of blessing, than when the summer sun of 1849 shone upon them. Peace, prosperity, and health, were theirs, thankfully received, and humbly enjoyed.

The Sabbath of July 22d, found Edwin, as usual, doing and getting good. The Sabbath-school and the house of God saw him at his post of duty, and place of worship. In the evening, the brothers sang together, as they often did; and in the following lines from a hymn of Charles Wesley, their voices seemed to rise with more than common fervor and devotion:

"How happy every child of grace
  Who knows his sins forgiven :
This earth, he cries, is not my place,
  I seek my place in heaven,
A country far from mortal sight ;
  Yet O, by faith I see
The land of rest, the saint's delight,
  The heaven prepared for me.

Then let me *suddenly* remove,
  That hidden life to share ;
I shall not lose my friends above,
  But more enjoy them there.
There we in Jesus' praise shall join,
  His boundless love proclaim ;
And solemnize in songs divine,
  The marriage of the Lamb."

The father, about leaving the room at the beginning of the second verse, lingered at the door deeply affected, and awed by the new beauty and significance which the words and the music seemed to possess. There was an expression in Edwin's voice which showed his own soul kindling in sympathy with the feelings of the pious poet.

On Thursday evening, he was at his class-meeting, a meeting for prayer and religious fellowship, and when asked if he could testify that he was assuredly born again, made a child of God and heir of heaven, "I feel thankful," he answered humbly, "that I do know that I am a child of God. I have had in the past week seasons of communion with him, and desire more constantly to realize his presence, and live to his glory."

Two days after this, Edwin was dead; he died of cholera. How did the father bear this heavy stroke?

"The moment he either saw or felt the rod," his minister tells us, "'*I* have sinned' was on his lips, or in the depths of his heart. The dread evening when his beloved son was writhing in the grasp of the disease, leaving him in other hands, he meets his class, and then takes a poor intelligent pious man, a local preacher, 'his own son in the faith,' and returns in darkness to the lone summer-house in his extensive lawn, and they long continued wrestling together, 'with strong crying and tears;' the personal dread of *His* wrath who is 'glorious in holiness,' absorbing the anguish of the parent's natural affection. Returning in the advanced night to his afflicted dwelling, with the cry, My sins, *my sins* are the cause of all this!' his pious children gather around him, and all in succession, from the oldest to the youngest, are heard pleading with God for their father's consolation and ·deliverance. This piercing apprehension of the evil of sin, with the powerfully healing balm of divine grace, given preeminently in answer to the 'prayer of faith,' prepared him and his family for such a manifestation of piety as I do not recollect ever to have witnessed.

"A few days afterwards, returning from the conference, expecting on entering his dwelling to enter a cloud 'whose darkness might be felt,' what was my surprise to find it a true dwelling of an Israelite, 'all *light within.*' The darkness was outside; here they all walked in the light of the Lord, and all tears were wiped from every eye. I beheld, and was edified. I wondered, and shall never forget. ' Mr. Budgett not only murmured not, but was ceaseless in praises that he and his family had been dealt with so mercifully. I knew how he loved his son, and what he expected from him."

"We are yet, though suffering under a most painful bereavement, a happy family," Mr. Budgett himself says; "yes, the peace of God, that passeth all human understanding, does keep our hearts and minds through faith in Jesus Christ. It would be impossible to tell you how precious Christ is to us in this time of severe trial. We have this morning enjoyed a gracious visitation from our heavenly Father, while we all, the whole family, knelt and prayed that this stroke might be fully sanctified."

Thus was gladness put into his heart "more than in the time that his corn and his wine increased."

But the separation between the father and son was not to be measured by years. In a little more than a year, the shadow of death again crept over this household. *We* would stay its progress, and pray for the continuance of such a life; but our times are in His hand who killeth and maketh alive, who woundeth and healeth.

In November of 1850, Mr. Budgett's health began to decline; for some months disease slowly but surely crept into, and fastened itself upon his once vigorous and stout frame. It was dropsy. Week by week, and day by day, he failed. Though its progress was sometimes slackened, it was never stopped. The winter he passed without much physical suffering, and he welcomed once more the opening beauties of the spring, but he was then hastening to a spring of immortal green.

"When I look round on my family and the church, I feel as if life would still be a blessing," says the sick merchant. "I am not one of those who are weary of the world, nor do I feel any sympathy with such; but when I look at myself as an individual, I feel 't were better to go.

"'There is my house, my portion fair,
My treasure and my heart are there,
And my abiding home.'

"But I did not feel like this at the beginning of my sickness; then I felt my own unfaithfulness had been so great, I wished to be spared a few years longer, that I might better prepare for heaven; but I have been led to see I could do nothing to *merit* heaven.

"'In my hand no price I bring,
Simply to thy cross, I cling.'

I trust now in the merits of my Saviour, in his atoning blood. I feel that it is not by works of righteousness which we have done, but of his mercy hath he saved us."

"I have passed a pleasant night, but feel myself getting weaker," he again says. "My stay on earth will be short. I shall soon arrive at home It gives me great pleasure to think we shall be an unbroken family in heaven. My father's family are many of them gone; the rest are on the way. A part of my own family are in heaven. Oh, how thin does the veil now appear which separates earth from heaven."

Are his worldly affairs in order?

"I have not a paper to sign, not a shilling to give away, not a book but any one may understand in ten minutes," he answers. "I feel as if I were a poor sinner, saved through my dear mother's prayers, the prayers of my friends, and my own poor feeble prayers offered through Christ. He cannot cast me off, but has gently guided me through the wilderness, and is keeping me there till I am perfected through suffering."

"In the vigor of life, how hard to bring our minds to believe we must suffer. But the Lord has brought me to a death-bed, and I this day," he says, with a sweet trust, "hang like a little child in a brook, catching hold of a branch that is thrown out to save it, only there is this one difference in my case: I hang upon the *branch of Jesse's stem.* Christ will keep me. I am safe."

. "Do you feel that your heavenly Father can make you enjoy affliction?" asked a friend by his bedside.

"O yes; I do now," expresses the ripening saint. "I do n't feel myself like a sick man; I feel that I am luxuriating in God's presence. The room seems *filled* with God. So calm, so beautiful." Then did he unconsciously slide into prayer: "Lord, I am thine; thou art mine. I have made a covenant with thee; I would not break it for a thousand worlds. Lord, keep me, baptize me anew; help me to rejoice more fully in thee.

> "Jesus, my great High-priest,
>   Offered his blood, and died;
> My guilty conscience seeks
>   No sacrifice beside.
> His powerful blood did once atone,
> And now it pleads before the throne."

Talking one day with the young wife of his son James: "I should like to have lived a little longer for your sake. Sometimes I feel as if I should like to look forward and trace your course through life. But I can, and do com-

mend you to the care of our heavenly Father.
He will guide you aright. Oh, 'in all your
ways acknowledge him, and he will direct your
steps.'" Looking earnestly at her, he said,
"'Let your eye be single, then your body shall
be full of light:' mind, keep a single eye; in all
the events of life, keep a single eye." .

"You are entering life under very different
circumstances with regard to temporal things,
from what I did," he said to his son William,
one day; "pursue the same course that I have
done, and your way is made; but let there be
this difference: where I have followed trifles,
you follow the dictates of the Spirit; wherein
I have followed my senses, you cleave close to
God, and all will be well. I can't say with
the apostle, 'I have fought a good fight,' for I
have not. I have been unfaithful, but there is
atonement through Jesus. I can say, I have
almost 'finished my course;' henceforth there is
laid up for me a crown of righteousness, which
the Lord, the righteous Judge, shall give me at
that day."

On being told, after an evening service, how
fervently he had been prayed for, "Oh," he
said, "they will not have to pray for me again;

before another month goes round, I shall be in a better country." .

"How delightful," remarked a friend near, "is the thought that you will so soon be there. There you will have a harp of gold, be clothed in white raiment, and have a crown upon your head."

"Yes," responded the dying saint, "I like to hear of the beauties of heaven, but I do not *dwell* upon them; no, what I rejoice in is, that *Christ will be there.* Where he is, there shall I also be. I know that he is in me, and I in him. I shall see him as he is; I *delight in knowing that.*"

On Sunday, April 20, the communion was administered to him; and he ate the bread and drank the wine of the new covenant for the last time with his family on earth. It was a day of holy solemnities, and a foretaste of heavenly blessedness.

"This is the happiest day of my life," he whispered, as it drew to a close; "the happiest hour. I am ready to go this moment, or ready to stay. Oh, how would I preach, if I could preach now!"

"He bade his ministers an affectionate farewell," so writes a friend who was with him; and on one of them repeating the lines,

> "I the chief of sinners am,
> But Jesus died for me,"

he fervently responded to the sentiment, and added, "I never asked for joy; I always thought myself unworthy of it; but he has given me more than I asked."

"He giveth exceeding abundantly, above all we ask or think," said one.

"Thank God, thank God," ejaculated the dying believer. After the ministers retired, he requested another hymn might be sung. On Edwin's favorite being selected, "How happy every child of grace," he said, "Yes; and Edwin will join us." He united most heartily in the singing, and desired another hymn, when it was thought too much excitement might hurt him.

"Oh, no," he said; "nothing will hurt me now, I am going home; nothing can hurt me now."

He lingered a week longer in close and delightful communion with his Lord, ready to abide his will, and then went home to the Beloved of his soul.

Samuel Budgett died April, 1851, aged 57.

His family lost a father whom they delighted to honor; Kingswood Hill, a godly neighbor, and a generous friend; Bristol, a princely merchant; the church of Christ, a shining member; England, a Christian citizen; but the world has found a new evangelist, who shall go forth in her highways and by-ways, to the shop and the counting-room, to the master and his men, to the poor and the rich, to preach, by his example, with no common power, the duty of laboring for Christ as the great *Bible law* of increase in temporal, moral, and spiritual good.

"The hand of the diligent maketh rich."

"Whatsoever thy hand findeth to do, *do it* with thy might."

"*Strive* to enter in at the strait gate; for many shall seek to enter in, and shall not be able."

"*Work* out your own salvation with fear and trembling; for it is God who worketh in you, to will and to do of his own good pleasure."

The American Tract Society

PUBLISH A LARGE SELECTION

OF

THE MOST CHOICE PRACTICAL WORKS

IN THE

ENGLISH LANGUAGE;

EMBODIED IN THE

RELIGIOUS (OR PASTOR'S) LIBRARY,
25 Vols. $10.

EVANGELICAL FAMILY LIBRARY,

15 Vols. $5 50.
And the continuation comprising 21 Vols. $7 50.

BESIDES

MORE THAN ONE THOUSAND

Books and Tracts for Old and Young,

MANY OF THEM

BEAUTIFULLY ILLUSTRATED.

Memoirs

LATELY PUBLISHED

BY THE

AMERICAN TRACT SOCIETY.

REV. JEREMIAH HALLOCK,

REV. PHILIP HENRY,

WILLIAM TUTTLE,

LADY HUNTINGTON AND HER FRIENDS,

MRS. MARTHA SHERMAN.

ALSO

ISABELLA GRAHAM, HARRIET L. WINSLOW,

SARAH L. HUNTINGTON SMITH,

DR. PAYSON, JAMES BRAINERD TAYLOR,

NORMAND SMITH,

AND

HARLAN PAGE.

AND

A GREAT VARIETY

OF

NARRATIVES FOR THE YOUNG,

BEAUTIFULLY ILLUSTRATED.

THE FAMILY TESTAMENT,

With brief Notes and Instructions, and Maps.

PREPARED BY REV. JUSTIN EDWARDS, D. D.

With the counsel and aid of the Members of the Publishing Committee.

Price 60 cents, or 80 gilt.

OLD TESTAMENT, Vol. I. Genesis to Job.   75 cents.

SACRED SONGS

For Family and Social Worship.

Selected by Prof. HASTINGS, with the counsel of LOWELL MASON, Esq., for general and permanent use; containing 320 hymns, and 182 tunes; 12mo, 55 cents.

SONGS OF ZION.

A smaller selection of 93 favorite tunes with hymns, which is gaining a wide circulation; 25 cents.

THE GENERAL SERIES OF TRACTS,

Is issued in a new edition of twelve volumes, with fine engravings.   Price $6 00.

THIRTEEN PACKETS OF SELECT TRACTS

Are also issued in a convenient form for booksellers and others, at 25 cents a Packet of 376 pages each

PICTORIAL NARRATIVES.

Twenty-four Tracts selected for the masses of readers; 248 pages, 12mo, 35 cents, or 50 gilt.

American Tract Society,

NEW YORK, 150 NASSAU-STREET; BOSTON, 28 CORNHILL; PHILADELPHIA, 303 CHESTNUT-STREET.

ImTheStory.com

Personalized Classic Books in many genre's

Unique gift for kids, partners, friends, colleagues

Customize:

- Character Names
- Upload your own front/back cover images (optional)
- Inscribe a personal message/dedication on the
  inside page (optional)

Customize many titles Including
- Alice in Wonderland
- Romeo and Juliet
- The Wizard of Oz
- A Christmas Carol
- Dracula
- Dr. Jekyll & Mr. Hyde
- And more...

CPSIA information can be obtained
at www.ICGtesting.com
Printed in the USA
BVHW041035160519
548477BV00015B/1186/P